重為輕根

靜為躁君

讀書隨錄

壽芝珍藏

【印】

frontspiece: Quotation from the Lao Tzu

Gravity is the Root of Lightness
Stillness the Ruler of Motion
Wholeness Combines Stillness and Motion
Expression and Calm, Sound and Silence.

The Art of
Playing the Piano
Conversations with Mortimer Markoff

The Art of
Playing the Piano
Conversations with Mortimer Markoff

by
Mortimer Markoff
and Frederic W. Platt

1993 • London Road Books • London • Palo Alto

Calligraphy by I-Tan Niu and Paul Price
Support from Artemas, Tom Devine and all my students
Translation by Charles Ridley
Design by London Road Design

Printed in the United States of America

London Road Books
535 Ramona Street, Suite 33
Palo Alto, California 94301

Library of Congress Cataloging-in-Publication Data
Markoff, Mortimer, 1920 –
The art of playing the piano: conversations with Mortimer Markoff
/by Mortimer Markoff and Frederic W. Platt.
p.   cm.
1. Piano--Performance. 2. Markoff, Mortimer, 1920– - Interviews.
I. Platt, Frederic W.
MT220.M275   1993
786.2'193--dc20
ISBN 0-9639221-7-3   93-38483
                                                     CIP
                                                      MN

This book is dedicated to all who understand that music is a resonant reflection of our existence.

—*Mortimer Markoff*

In Appreciation

I want to acknowledge all that Fred Platt has done
to make this book possible. Without Fred's energy,
persistence and infinite patience there would be
no book. I am deeply grateful to Fred and to his
wife, Connie, for her help as advisor and critic.
My profound thanks to both.

M.M.

Foreword

I was fortunate to meet Mortimer Markoff in 1960. He became my teacher and my friend. As a child I studied piano but had little understanding of what I was doing. Years later, reading Mann's *Buddenbrooks*, I began to see creating music was central, and mechanically perfect piano playing was secondary.

In 1960, I was attending medical school. Despite my crowded schedule, I rented a piano and set about finding a teacher. My wife knew a friend who recommended Mortimer Markoff. I called, explaining what I wanted and began studying with Mort. Now, thirty years later, I am still grateful for his gift of music and for his friendship.

After my medical training was completed in 1964, we left California. I saw Mort in 1975 for an infrequent lesson. Then I heard from him in 1988. He was writing an

Aesthetic of Pianism ... but with difficulty. Then I remembered Mort's special gifts: Incisive practical suggestions that enable one to improve dramatically, coupled with theories about every aspect of pianism. I never understood some of his concepts, but I've treasured every one of them. I thought, if I helped Mort produce a book, I would come to a better understanding of music. Many long distance conversations between Denver and Palo Alto followed, and eventually this book evolved.

    Mort and I hope these conversations are enlightening. My role throughout was to hear Mort, to understand him, and when confused, to ask for clarification. If I have left some questions unasked, I beg the reader's pardon.

Fred Platt

Preface

In the beginning I played the piano with only musical instinct to guide me. Though fortunate to have had distinguished teachers, my standards were entirely my own and, though I could not explain them, I seldom questioned my own judgement.

I wrote down concepts and insights that seemed useful in notebooks I kept even before I began to teach others. Over years these evolved into a whole aesthetic of pianism unlike any I had seen. The parallel to aspects of Eastern thought became clear only later.

I taught, at first, as I played, out of instinct. Soon I saw that the concepts were powerful tools for teaching. Students quickly progressed beyond playing the right notes at the right time and would, at whatever level, make music moving and musical. Although one's own musical nature is fundamental, it will be expressed more surely if it is part of a whole view of pianism.

Such an overview involves fundamental new concepts you may never have considered. Be encouraged,
for the naive pianist, or even the beginner, will learn new
concepts more quickly than the advanced pianist who is
committed to long established practice and routine.

These concepts, rightly understood and used,
will transform perception and playing. At best, whether
less advanced or an artist, you will be enabled to lift your
playing to the highest level. There it may end, where it
might have begun: Simply, with an honest expression.

M.M.

Contents

The Art of Playing the Piano

The highest aim is to make the music speak.
~ Pablo Casals

FP   Mort, as a pianist, what do I really have to know? I once thought the job consisted of simply playing the notes, counting, and curving my fingers.

MM   Well, it helps to understand what your task is at the piano. You are re-creating an expressive design out of tone and within time. The material you use is tone, and your canvas is a silent time space. You paint your design with tone on a silent but moving canvas of time. The more whole, complete, and integrated the design is, the better it will be; however, you must discover for yourself the sense of the whole design. As students, we are usually given few concepts to help us, nor do we learn to trust our own musical instinct. Many pianists believe that there is an authority to tell them "how it goes," never having discovered that an authentic performance comes from one's own honest response to the music. To play well, learn to trust your own musical nature. You may discover this early, but some pianists never find this out. Only the music can speak for itself, so you must think and feel what the music demands.

FP   How do I manage that?

MM   There are three elements to consider. First, and most important, is an awareness of time. Time contains rhythm and is the medium for all music. Second is tone, the material for music. Third is the melodic line that you draw while moving within time, and so create a musical shape.

FP   I control these elements?

MM   Yes, you do. The distinguishing qualities in a great performance are unity and wholeness, together with an honest expression. And you can't achieve this by intellect alone. Heart and head are both involved. Feeling will determine what the expression and character of a work should be, but thought will guide you. And it must be a direct expression, not calculated or contrived. The element of spontaneity or inspiration is a necessary part of every beautiful performance. Even if you are a great artist, you will not be able to re-create an ideal performance each time you play a work.

FP   In summary, I must be quite aware of time, tone, and line.

MM   Yes, to think the music clearly, you need a con-
ception of the materials of music and how they go
together to create the musical design. First, establish an
awareness of the flow of time or duration even before a
tone is sounded. Duration supercedes and includes the
count. Thinking duration, or continuity, allows you to
relate the material in hand to the large design. When
duration is compelling, a remarkable change occurs. Your
perception and the music are both transformed. Second,
you need to hold your material, the tone, by careful listening, touching, and relaxing. An honest tone demands
the closest association between touch, time, and the
tone itself. Finally, there is the melodic line, the most
prominent feature of the design. The line must be clear,
coherent, and convincing.

If duration or continuity is strong, the music will
be moving. If the tone is honest, and tone and touch
match, the result will be touching. If the line is unbroken
and energy sustained, the design will be clear.

These three elements are basic for a beautiful
performance.

2

The Musical Design

That was playing that was integrated and whole and moreover had good continuity.

~ Ludwig Beethoven

FP   Mort, can you first tell me what you mean by the musical design?

MM   I mean the composition as a whole. That will be the shape and the sense that you create out of tone in time. Expression and design, or shape and content, are one and the same. You express the music, not yourself. The task is not self-expression.

FP   Is that an important issue? The pianist expressing music, not the self?

MM   Very important. If affects your entire relation to the music and the work. If you are subjective and too involved, to that degree you are blind to the expression in the music. A good attitude is expressed by Bertolt

Brecht's term, *Verfremdung*, translated as "estrangement" or "detachment." Not cool or removed, but from
a vantage point that allows the music to be yet more
expressive.

FP   The pianist needs a certain detachment?

MM   Right. In the words of Herrigel's Zen archer,
"egoless." And that makes a great difference and allows
a more genuine emotional response.

FP   Mort, do you see a lack of detachment as a common student problem?

MM   Yes. And not only for students. If you are too subjective you are overcome by your own feelings. This prevents a simple direct response to the music. Expression
is the shape of the music itself. Shape and content are
the same. The title of the book by Ben Shahn, the
painter, *The Shape of Content*, nicely makes that point.
When both form and content match, the music has a self-
contained energy, and the music, not the performer, will
dictate the expression.

FP   Will that lead to a uniform production of each
piece?

MM   No, you will be projecting the music through yourself. But, since perception differs for every occasion and
for each person, every interpretation will reveal a different
aspect of the same work. Actually, the most genuine
expression of the self will occur when you are selfless.

FP   All right then. I am to attempt to allow the music to express itself. What next? How do I look at the musical design?

MM   Consider three vantage points: the near view, the middle view, and the whole view. Begin by considering the whole view, the most inclusive: that is, an awareness of the flow of time. This sense of time is what I call duration. That, more than anything else, will draw the other elements into place. Duration makes things whole.

FP   You intend "wholeness" to be my goal then.

MM   Absolutely.

FP   And to achieve that wholeness, I must be aware of the flow of time.

MM   Yes. I think to hear a good Richter recital is to be convinced. There is a sense of wholeness, viewing the entire work as a whole, not the sum of little parts. Neuhaus, Richter's teacher, rightly ascribed it to his unique sense of rhythm. He used the phrase "time-rhythm," which is to say the rhythm of time. Beethoven meant the same when he said that the best playing was "integrated and whole and, moreover, had good continuity." Continuity is the condition for making it whole. Continuity in time is the definition for duration. When thinking duration, you are better able to perceive relationship. Whether the music is loud or soft, slow or fast, an awareness of duration or time as a constant flow is crucial.

FP   Mortimer, this is happening anyway. The flow of time goes on whether you notice it or not.

MM   Absolutely. But a good performance makes time's passage deeply felt. The flow of time is so much a condition of our existence that we are seldom aware of it. If a fish were asked how it feels to live in water, he'd say, "Let me see, I've never been out of water." We've never been out of time and when we drop dead, it will be too late to report. Being conscious of the flow of time transforms perception and enlivens it. An acute awareness of time's flow will seem to slow time and to provoke such statements as "time seemed to stand still." It is as if you were in a stream moving with the current so that a leaf close by on the water would seem to be still.

FP   Going with the flow is a Californian concept.

MM   Well, some good things come from California.

FP   The large view, in the re-creation of the musical design, then grows from the sense of time itself.

MM   Exactly.

FP   Then what? As you sit at the piano experiencing the flow of time, what do you do next?

MM   You concentrate on retaining and strengthening this awareness. The first tone must be a continuation, not a beginning, because that would be a denial of time's flow. At every moment, each tone and every phrase is heard in relation to the omnipresent sense of time, and every tone must be a confirmation of time's flow. Music itself is the expression of duration, or continuance, in time.

FP   I have a picture of someone sitting at the piano with a vivid sense of the flow of time, conducting the flow with appropriate gesture, and not getting anywhere near the keys.

MM   Absolutely. That's a very good image for the middle view and a way to practice the *gest, or the phrase motion. Actually, you are conducting yourself. You move, within limits, with the wrist and the forearm, as a conductor's arm moves. As with a good conductor, there will be the sense of the larger rhythm—duration itself—and within that, the smaller motion, the gest, that creates the phrase.

FP   Is this body English?

MM   Maybe body Music, a more universal language than body English. It points out the basic relation that music has to dance and movement. The roots for music are in moving and speaking and, on another level, dancing and singing.

FP   OK. When are we going to get to the piano?

* Gest: an expressive gesture, to bear, to carry, to conduct. Relative to the German "Gestalt:" form, shape, a whole constituting more than the sum of the parts. From Webster's Unabridged 2nd Edition.

MM   We should talk about touch. That's the near view. Your material is tone, individual tone, and the tones as they are combined. At the piano you have to get a tone by means of this button, the key. The problem is that the key is not close to the string. You can't touch a tone. A Rube Goldberg mechanism intervenes between your fingertips and the point where the hammer touches the string. Your hand is quite distant from the tone. You have to make a very clear mental association between tone and touch. It is the mental association between the tone, the key, and the touch that makes tone and touch match. We say "that was touching" when we mean close or immediate. It is the function of touch to create the tone. There are other concerns. It is not easy to listen to a piano tone. The ear will tend to reject the percussive noise, or thump, that precedes the tone itself. I call it the hit.

FP   Do you mean the thud of the key or the hit of the hammer?

MM   The hit of the hammer. You must learn to listen to the hit as part of the tone. The tone actually begins before the key comes to a stop. Avoid going too deep into the key, what Matthay called "key bedding," that is, pressing past the point where the key stops. Though the key will usually travel past the point where the tone begins, aim for that spot. Does that leave too much unspoken about what I call touch and tone? The relaxed condition whereby you get the best tone.

FP   The relaxed condition?

MM   Well, you see, it is most important to be totally relaxed. Chopin said, "Flexibility is everything." I realize that you cannot do anything but fall off the piano bench if you are too relaxed. But if you perform an action of any kind with the least possible tension, you will have done it most efficiently.

FP   Let's see. As a pianist just past the novice level, I am sitting at the piano, thinking about the flow of time, swooping about in a gesture that will fit the design, am totally relaxed as I strike the tones, . . .

MM   Don't even think of striking. You should strike the word "strike." Rather think that you are in touch. Be touching the key even before you touch the tone. Pretend that the finger is limp all the way up the shoulder and you intend the tone where you aim the key, as if an electric current goes to that spot where the tone begins. You really don't think of depressing, let alone striking. That would be like closing a door by striking it, a waste of energy. If the touch is right, you get an honest tone.

FP   OK, let's go over this again. Just how do you get this "honest tone?"

MM   First, you should listen to the beginning of the tone very consciously because the ear wants to reject the noise made by the hit. Second, touch the key in advance, and be very aware of touch at the moment of the hit. Third, approach and move the key with a totally relaxed body, arm, wrist, and fingers.

FP   With these components, the flow of time, the gesture for line and the honest touch, what have we gotten to?

MM   The necessary steps for a fine production. And these are the three levels to examine if something seems wrong. You ask, "Is it the tone?" or "Is it the rhythm overall?" You'll know where you have gone awry and be able to correct the problem. Usually you can find where the difficulty might be, and how to correct it.

FP   Does this presuppose that we have mastered playing the right notes, at the right time, and in the right order?

MM   It does, except there isn't a time when you should practice getting the right notes without time. After all, if you practice the notes out of time, you practice something else. The concession you make is going slowly enough, perhaps isolating each hand or each voice. In this way, you learn more rapidly. If you learn notes without any shape, it is much more difficult.

FP   That sense of the group of notes as a shape.

MM   Yes. I call that shape the line, and you create the line with the right gest.

FP   Can you summarize these thoughts about musical design?

MM   I can try. When playing the piano, we are re-creating a design out of tone, our material. With tone and the gest, we form the line, the musical shape. Within time, that is duration, we can order, proportion, and relate the various elements and so find meaning or expression. The design is complete when it is time-full, tone-full, and tune-full.

FP   What else should I understand under the topic of the Musical Design?

MM   Well, I would include attitude. Attitude is your relation to music and the piano, both physical and mental. How you sit, loosely, but not tucked into yourself, with the forearms even with the keyboard, the knees just under, and so on. Your mental attitude is even more important.

FP   And of all this, you say that the most important is the flow of time?

MM   Yes. Once that is established, you come back to listening to the silence, and finally, to complete calm. And then play in such a way as not to disturb either. A child will be able to play in such a way; an adult will have more difficulty, and an advanced pianist might not get it at all.

FP   All right, and I understand that this tripartite scheme helps if you are dissatisfied with your performance. Is there anything else that helps?

MM   Well, the concept of energy helps. I like Webster's definition of energy as "strength of expression" because it is neutral. So I say play with energy, meaning expression. A decrease in the energy is an indication of a problem.

FP   What is it that seems to lack energy? The pianist or the piece?

MM   The pianist is the intermediary, and the piece is the result. It is the music itself that has to reflect energy. And that energy may be in many areas, but listening to a work with energy in mind tells you a great deal. If the energy is sustained, the performance is on the right track.

FP   So then one way of monitoring whether the piece is going well . . .

MM   Monitoring is the right word.

FP   . . . is to have a sense of whether or not the piece maintains the right energy. If it lacks energy, you know something is wrong. O.K. Then you say to yourself, if something is wrong, it is probably a problem of the tone, or the line, or of time. How do I decide which?

MM   I think you have to make an educated guess. The first thing is to check from the large to the small. If there is a compelling rhythm, I tend to think it makes all other things right but, if not that, then you have to examine the line. The line may be lacking in tension. The line is a fundamental musical expression of energy. If that is all right and there seems to be a strong gesture, and it moves within the big arc of time itself, then you have to move down and ask if the tone itself has sufficient energy.

FP   Do you think this is accessible to the pianist

alone or more to a teacher? Do you use this analysis as a teacher?

MM   Yes, I do. But the point is that the teacher helps the student learn to listen. Learning to listen is what it is all about.

FP   Do you mean that teaching piano is not so much teaching to play as it is teaching to listen?

MM   I think that is saying it very well.

3

Establishing the Ground

Gravity is the root of lightness and stillness the ruler of motion.
~ Lao Tzu

FP   Mort, would you say again what you think is the
most important element in the best music playing?

MM   The ability to create the "ground" for music,
which is the ability to hear and play . . . nothing! The
ground for tone or sound is silence; the ground for
motion is stillness, and the ground for expression is calm
or "no expression." Yet this ground is more than a clean
slate. It is analogous to the white space in a traditional
Oriental painting that is half the picture.

FP   But you wouldn't say that the ground or the
white space was the essential idea, would you?

MM   Who is to say which half of the tonal painting is
the more expressive? In a fine black and white study, one

half would not exist without the other. Being aware of both halves heightens perception and makes the whole design stronger. Fritjof Capra quotes the Buddhist *sutras* as saying, "Form is emptiness and emptiness is form."

FP   This is a little too abstract for me. Are we talking about silence? Or about the music you play?

MM   We are speaking of both. Nor is it abstract. One would not be without the other. Mozart, when asked what was the most beautiful effect in music, replied, "No music." Too good an answer, I believe, to be apocryphal. The way to establish the ground is by means of a strong rhythm. Not the usual idea of rhythm, but the sense of pure duration.

FP   All right. But if establishing the ground is the most important, I want to ask you if your view has changed from the time I studied with you thirty years ago. At that time, when I asked you what the most important goal was, you said, "To play the line." Do you no longer think that?

MM   Yes, I still think so. But without destroying the ground. Pursuing the line should not preclude the other elements I described.

FP   Hmmm. What do you do with the silence?

MM   I listen to it as closely as to the sound. It is the ground for music. And it is most important to be able to create that clean slate. The ability to hear and play nothing. Silence and sound are equally important.

FP   I have trouble concentrating on the nothing when I could be focusing on something.

MM   On the contrary, the "something" will be much clearer to you. The way, maybe the only way, to establish the ground is by means of a strong rhythm, which comes from the sense of pure duration.

FP   Well, Mort, if you think that, I would say to you, "Please play the ground for a while so I can see how I like it." After a while I'd say, "I'm finding it a fairly boring piece. Could you please play something else?" How can you think that the ground is as important as the line itself?

MM   It's not more important, but it is just as important. It is half the piece.

FP   But if a good pianist was able to establish the ground perfectly well, and never play a thing, you'd never know he was a pianist at all.

MM   Do you know the piece by John Cage called *Silence*? I remember the article in the *New Yorker* years ago about the performance of this work. There was a question of separating the movements since the pianist was just sitting at the piano. He would close the fall board and then open it up for the second movement. The last movement was distinguished by the "restive muttering in the audience." I will always remember that phrase. I loved it. I'm sure that "restive muttering" created a different piece. Cage was making a point, after all.

FP   I can imagine that if it was four pages long, it could be *allegretto*, but if it were two pages you could play it *adagio* and it would sound like four pages played *allegretto*.

MM   There are those subtleties.

FP   Yes. I think that if I play a nice melody, but rushed, perhaps with not very good control of the ground . . .

MM   You would know it.

FP   I would know it, and I would say the silence was not very good, but I still like that little piece. On the other hand, if I played silence with perfect control of the ground, I wouldn't have heard any piece at all.

MM   But you might have been very peaceable. One of the roots of the word "music" is "muse", meaning "to meditate in silence." A meditative state for music is not overstating the case, and it does relate to what we have said about detachment.

FP   Where do the line and the tones fit on the ground? If our goal is to listen to the silence and to be careful not to disturb it, how do we place the line on this canvas of silence?

MM   That's exactly the problem; one defines the other. One must play the line without disturbing that perception of silence, stillness, and calm.

FP   Does it bother you that getting ready to play Chopin is exactly the same as getting ready to play Prokofiev? Or anyone else?

MM   No.

FP   But there must be a tiny unit of time in which the pianist switches from being ready to play *anything* to being ready to play *something* unique.

MM   Right.

FP   What happens?

MM   It seems to me that you must begin to think of a specific style and a more specific expression, the central idea perhaps. For example, it seems to me that playing Scarlatti presupposes the cleanest slate. A pristine, open space. There is a kind of fresh and naive light in the space. I think that holds very well for Scarlatti.

FP   Do you mean that the ground is different for Scarlatti than for someone else?

MM   No, the ground is not different here; it is just more apparent. There is more open space.

FP   So it is fair to say that the ground is exactly the same for every piece of music.

MM   That's right. That's what we said before anyone in particular came on the scene, and if you then begin to talk about a specific composer, you must talk about the relationship of that particular line to the ground. With Scarlatti, the line is so fine that there is more white space. And because there is more of it, it's already different. As contrasted, I was going to say, with Debussy, where the ground is almost as veiled as the sound.

FP   It sounds as if a change occurs to the ground when you begin to place the line in it.

MM   Well, I think maybe that is implicit in the notion that half of a picture is the painting and the other half is the white space. If I draw a single thin line, I've created more white space than if I draw a very thick line. I can't touch one without touching the other. Although the white space is neutral at first, its significance changes according to the design. Finally, you will come to realize that the ground is as expressive, often more expressive, than the sound. A silence can be perfect, but it is hard to produce a perfect sound.

4

Duration

Such a complete whole of nature we call a 'duration.'
~ Alfred North Whitehead

FP   Mort, what is the relationship between playing
the line and rhythm?

MM   The rhythm *is* the relationship! You would not be
able to relate one part of the line to another without a
sense of time, let alone relate other elements in a
composition. Music cannot exist outside of time. Nor can
we, as a matter of fact. The expression of time, or
duration, is fundamental to music and music-making. I
am not talking about the beat when I say rhythm. The
beat can help organize the detail, but it is undivided time
that allows you to grasp the whole shape. The beat is the
way we measure time. And we need to measure it
because that enables us to keep things in proportion.
Although counting may make things mathematically
correct, it doesn't of itself, create a sense of coherence

and meaning. That can only be gained by a larger view, that is, by the sense of time itself.

FP   Why so much focus on the flow of time? Why not start with the music itself? Can't we adjust our rhythm later?

MM   That would be getting it backward. Music exists in time. It is an expression of time, so to order it you must play in time. It helps to consider the framework for other media. A sculptor who works with clay has an armature. A painter has a canvas stretched on a frame. A weaver has the warp and woof of his loom. But the difficulty and the wonder of creating a musical design is that you must spin in thin air with an impalpable material, tone. You could say that the musician weaves with tone on a loom of time. Instead of stretched strings you have the beat, marking the flow of time. The beat is the traditional framework for music, and, indeed, with the beat you are able to measure the time-space and retain a sense of proportion. However, the beat is only the measure of time's flow, and it alone cannot establish continuity. The sense of flow, or the expression of time, is the key. Forgive the pun.

FP   There are some kinds of music where the beat does seem to be a central part of the design, for example, rock music.

MM   That's true. And, because the beat is so central in the design, we think it is the beat that creates rhythm, but it's the other way around. It is not the beat that creates rhythm, it's the sense of motion which is reflected in a very prominent beat as in a march or in much popular music. The beat is an integral part, but I can demonstrate that only expressing the beat, even in a march, wouldn't satisfy you. There must be continuity as well as the beat. Is that clear?

FP   Getting clearer. Does a metronome help with rhythm?

MM   Almost the opposite. The metronome is used to determine tempo and to indicate a regular pulse. It is incapable of expressing continuity. In fact, you may hear it saying, "stop, stop, stop." What you need to hear is "go, go." The way I play the march that seems so unsatisfactory says, "stop, stop." But that's the expression of the beat alone and that is musically unsatisfactory. It is a denial of music.

FP   So we must establish the flow of time and then play the notes at the proper time.

MM   Think of staying just behind the flow. Every tone has to reflect continuity or flow. Think *flow* first, then stay behind, so that you are always waiting. A strong rhythm creates suspense, a waiting in time, and by creating that waiting presence you reveal duration. Given a moment in time, how are you to judge when you should play the next note but by waiting? That's the simplest way to put it. If you strengthen the sense of waiting then everything is stronger.

FP   What are you waiting for?

MM   You are waiting for time's flow, the better to judge the moment for the next tone. I agree with Matthay who says to play each note "at the last possible moment."

FP   But you are going to be the one to play it!

MM   And, if the timing is good, you won't destroy the sense of waiting. You know listening is what it is all about. The Anglo-Saxon root of the word "to listen" is "*hlosian*," which means "to wait in suspense." This is more than a remarkable coincidence!

FP   Well, I am still confused. Mort, as I'm sitting there playing the piece, I play a tone and then I wait for the next one. How do I know when I'm ready to play it?

MM   By its relation to the beat, which is the measure of the flow of time, and by a constant waiting. You are given the formal structure of the measure, and you have spaced the beats evenly. Actually, you have no way of knowing what "even" is without having a prevailing constant, which is the passage of time. It really is a simple point, but it is difficult to make it clear.

FP   By always waiting and imagining that I am to play just behind the flow of time, am I implying that if I play the note at precisely the right time, it will be a little bit late?

MM   No. You may be playing metronomically, yet thinking of playing as I have described will change your perception of it. For example, I can play a little ahead of the flow and yet play with the metronome. The notes will match the clicks, but it will seem as if the metronome is hurrying. By staying with the imaginary flow, and yet playing with the metronome, it will seem slower. And if I imagine playing behind the flow, as every note sounds with the click, the music will seem as if it slowed even more. And I have no way of explaining this; however, I can demonstrate it with a little Schubert dance. In each case the music follows the metronome exactly, but with the flow it sounds slow, behind the flow slower still, and without flow, faster, yet all in the same tempo.

FP   As I hear these examples played on the piano, I wonder if the real difference is the incorporation of an overall gesture.

MM   I think not. This way of thinking time or duration influences everything so profoundly that gesture, tone, and expression are all affected, which is exactly what you would like it to do.

FP   Are there other routes to the same end? Can I reach the same goal by feeling the flow, or by playing the line, or by establishing the right gesture?

MM   Yes and no. All these elements are closely linked, so if you push any one element to the limit—color, for instance,—you would come to the ideal. But I believe the all-inclusive element that brings all others in its train is duration.

FP   Surely there are some pieces where your patience is more tested by the flow. For example, the little B minor *landler* of Schubert. Is the sense of flow more inherent in that piece?

MM   Almost any very slow movement is always more difficult to sustain. You could say that some pieces are so bound in time that you are driven to discover the rhythm that will sustain them.

FP   Mort, when we first met, I said that I wanted to learn music rather than piano. You said that was your approach. I'm wondering if you are moving more toward pianistic technique now.

MM   Certainly not, because the emphasis on music is still my approach; only now it is more inclusive. My teaching is anything but limited to piano technique, but it is much clearer as to what constitutes an adequate technique.

FP   If this sense of duration or flow helps the playing, does it help one glean any more in listening to performances? Does it alter how one hears, make one more critical?

MM   Yes, to all of those. It does make you more appreciative of a good performance and less tolerant of a bad one.

FP   What would you say if I stubbornly held out that the concept of the line helps me more than a sense of the flow of time?

MM   I would say that you understand line better than time. And it is easier to grasp the concept of the line. But let me read from the *New York Times* about Tim Mayotte, the tennis player. He accepted an upset as if it had been expected. "Not surprising," he said, "I'm not beating anyone. I don't feel like an instinctive player. There's no flow out there and that's really the problem." You see, *flow* is critical, and not only for pianists. I think that there is no magic touchstone, but if there was, it would be duration. What really matters most is the awareness of the passage of time.

FP   I am still a little confused about when to play the notes. I think I will sit at the piano and wait until the note wants to be played.

MM   That should do it.

5

Duration and Rhythm

Duration is rather the self-contained and therefore self-renewing movement of an organized, firmly integrated whole, taking place in accordance with immutable laws and beginning anew at every ending.
~ I-Ching

FP   How did you come to this concept of duration?

MM   Very gradually, over a long period of time. I knew that when playing was at its ideal musically, the rhythm was the determining thing, as if rhythm made all things right. I discovered that slow movements, difficult to sustain, could be made more gripping by concentrating on the space between distant beats. I would count "one" for a long slow measure, perhaps with an "and" in the middle, and "two and" for the next measure. So I had to wait intently. I began to see that the point was in the sense of waiting, the feeling of suspense. It became clear that intensifying the sense of waiting would lift my playing to a higher level. I came to see that waiting, the sense of suspense, is the feeling of time passing and that it was especially powerful in a great performance. Finally,

I realized the right word was duration, which means continuity-in-time. It is the sense of duration that creates the most powerful rhythm.

FP   To wait intently.

MM   Yes. About that time, Sviatoslav Richter made, in two consecutive years, his only San Francisco appearances. The first time I didn't think he played as well as his reputation would have led me to expect. The following year he gave two recitals in San Francisco, and they seemed to be a confirmation of everything I had thought about piano playing and especially about rhythm. The playing was engrossing. You were caught from the very beginning of the seldom-heard Schubert sonata. I had the sense that it was going before it began, and that it was always about to begin even after it had begun. Richter never lost that feeling. It was suspended; the listeners were suspended, spellbound, not only for the Schubert but for the entire recital. It was the most sustained and compelling piano recital I had ever heard.

FP   I can see that you became a fan of Richter's that day.

MM   Really. The recital was so good that I scrambled to get tickets to the second recital, quite a feat since it was already sold out. That too was a remarkable recital. It got off on its left foot, perhaps I should say left hand, with a totally erratic and wild first movement of a Mozart sonata, but then settled down with the second movement, and was in the end the best Mozart I had ever heard in recital. The rest of that performance was as remarkable as the first had been.

FP   To return to the subject of "duration," can you contrast that term to "rhythm?"

MM   Rhythm is a sub-category under duration. Duration is the inclusive word, meaning continuity-in-time. The term rhythm comes from the Greek *rhythmos*, meaning measured motion. Rhythm is concerned with movement, and the beat is the means for measuring that motion. I came to realize that the beat was not central. When I asked the violinist Mischa Elman for his definition of rhythm, he answered, "Well, we can agree that it's not the beat." I was very happy to hear that. It was a very satisfying answer for me.

FP   If rhythm is not the beat, but the measured motion that is governed by the flow of time, can we just do away with the beat?

MM   Not entirely. The function of the beat is to measure time. The beat segments time. It gives us equal portions of time, so we may more easily calculate proportion and place things in the right relation. That is a very important and integral part of the whole design; however, without the sense of flow, we wouldn't know if beats were spaced evenly. We may presume that flow is there, but believe me, it is not to be taken for granted. When we strengthen that sense of continuity, everything is transformed.

FP   If we strengthen continuity? How do we do that?

MM   We strengthen the sense of flow and our ability to visualize it. An image of time might be a great river. Another image can be produced by putting your arm up to 12 o'clock and drawing it down in a continuous sweeping motion, much like the movement of the second hand on a clock. If you ask someone to draw an image of the passing of time during a piece, using a moving arm, whether it is a fast or a slow tempo, and ask them to think not of tempo but of time, they bring that arm down at the same rate for any tempo, which suggests a universal constant, the flow of time.

FP   OK, let me see. I asked how you might strengthen the sense of continuity, and you suggested that one way would be to have that image of the sweep second hand.

MM   Or the whole arm, better. And let the arm move as smoothly and as energetically as you can. Not too fast; take at least fifteen seconds to go from twelve to six on your clock. And think as if you were conducting with that gesture and have it in your mind, or as you hum the music, have it go along in the train of that gesture.

FP   What happens if you pay more attention to the beat, to the subdivisions of the flow of time?

MM   That can be destructive to the sense of flow. However you can learn to count audibly so as to reflect suspense. One, . . . Two, . . . Three . . . Four. Then, when beginning to play, to continue counting with a voice indicating suspendedness. The beat can reflect continuity and suspense also. Then it's a very strong musical assistance. Don't drop the voice; the voice goes up at the end of each count and you think the space between the sharp, short syllables.

FP   As if they were connected by time.

MM   Exactly. It is the sense of time that makes the connection. Then it has a strong musical existence. It's a help, as it should be. Sometimes, instead of "One, two, three, four," I have people say, "*Wait*, two, three, four, *wait*, two three, four ..." to intensify the sense that the whole measure is a single block of time. Moving the beat further and further apart intensifies the sense of suspensefulness and creates the sense of pure duration.

FP   By the way, what is the function of the measure itself?

MM   The measure does what it says. It measures duration and groups the beat. It represents a block of time. Like a brick in a building, it is part of the rhythmic structure. The relation of the musical line to the measure determines your perception of that shape. For instance, if you consider a melody that ascends and then descends repeatedly and has the bar line at the beginning, then it looks and sounds like a melody that climbs and then falls. But if you move the bar line to the middle of the shape, to the high point, then it will sound like a figure that first falls, then climbs. We group measures as well as beats.

This reveals the sense of the whole shape. It is the grammer for music and is as important as the phrase.

FP   I've never understood that. Why not the whole piece without any measure markers?

MM   Well, in early music that was monophonic, that was the case. Gregorian chants, for example. The word held it all in place. It was much freer. But when contrapuntal music developed, there were different voices singing different melodies at the same time. There had to be some common denominator, and that was the measure. There are tensions that exist, and they are necessary and desirable. The grouping of measures does not necessarily conform to the phrase. The phrase often begins with an upbeat or in the middle of the measure and then crosses over the bar. And that creates a desirable tension. It makes it all the more cohesive and interesting.

FP   Ummm. If I understand right, rhythm and duration are the underlying ground or matrix for the music, and rhythm is the flow of time.

MM   Not the whole story of rhythm, but basic to it . . .

FP   And an awareness of it . . .

MM   . . . must be cultivated at any cost.

FP   And the function of the measure and the beat are to help us place things.

MM   Right.

FP   And to allow us to place different voices.

MM   That's how the measure evolved.

FP   And that to establish this sense of rhythm, of
flow, you have suggested images one could cultivate,
even the physical gesture. What then? When one is aware
of the flow of time, what does one do next?

MM   Well, I think that's the time to begin to play. Not
before. Then, at every turn, where the pattern changes,
where note values change, or the melodic pattern
changes, or any other event, at every turn you tell yourself "another pattern, same flow." New tempo, same flow!
A new movement even, same flow. You always are rein-
forcing that. I would say, "You are playing the expression
of duration." Since duration has, by definition, everything
to do with wholeness, you are doing everything you can
to make it whole. Duration is the means to
that end.

FP   OK. Could you tell me where you place the line
within the flow of time? Did you suggest that the line
comes just behind the flow of time, rather than right with
or ahead of it?

MM   It's the tone, not the line, that is to be played
slightly behind the flow of time. I'm not so certain that
you can speak of the line in quite the same way as you
can speak of the individual tone. The tone has a begin-

ning and an end. In a certain sense, a good line is endless. On one hand, you are dealing with points—that is,
notes—that have beginnings and endings. And with them
you're constructing a line that is in an endless space of
time.

FP   That's very lyrical, even if I don't understand it.
We've been talking about placing this musical line in the
flow of time, in duration.

MM   Let me put it another way. You are able to draw
the line, and you move as if you are as free as a bird in
drawing the phrase shape. But at a given moment, that
point on the line will match with our traditional beats.
A practical method for thinking of the line's relation to
time is to imagine that you are a little bit behind, or maybe very much behind the flow of time. All that does is
allow you to be totally prepared for each moment. And
your judgment of that moment will be the more accu-
rate, but it will seem unhurried. If hurry is the enemy
of rhythm, then deliberation is rhythm's friend.

FP   All right. I think I understand this emphasis on
the overall flow of time. I am willing to give up thinking
of all the other divisions, the beat, the measures, even
the phrases.

MM   Oh no, you can't do that. If you did you would
lose an important contradiction, the tension between the
flow of time and the music itself. You want to cultivate
and control that tension, for it is the bond that holds
everything together.

FP　　And phrasing?

MM　　Phrasing is a grouping that, of course, influences the line. It is a breath group. If you were playing a wind instrument or if you were singing, it would tell you when to take a breath. The phrases will often cross measures or include several measures.

FP　　So that again reminds us that the flow of time is one thing and the line is another.

MM　　Yes.

FP　　You really like these contradictions, don't you?

MM　　I think contradiction and resolution is central to any real understanding of music, and for that matter, the understanding of very many other things as well.

6

Melody, or "The Line"

We strive for a pure line—for the rest—an ideal sonority.
~ Wanda Landowska

FP   Mort, at one time, I remember asking you what I should do if I could only do one thing at a time. You replied that I should "play the line." Do you still believe that?

MM   Surely. The line is first, the first and last element of the design. The composer, at least in the past, started with a theme, a melody, a line. The line is basic.

FP   How do you build a line?

MM   First, I should explain what I mean by the musical line. I use that term to signify melody. The melody *is* the musical line. You create a line in music; the pianist draws an arm along the keyboard just as an artist draws the paintbrush along the canvas. Chopin used to demonstrate the scale by means of a *glissando*, which makes the same point, I think.

FP   What point?

MM   The point that line is created by gesture. Whether in music or dance, in drawing or painting, it is the sweep of the whole arm that creates the line.

FP   You mean that as a physical gesture, not a sound phenomenon?

MM   Absolutely. The one follows the other. If the gest is right, you will hear it, and if it is not there, you will feel it is missing in the music.

FP   So the line is equivalent to the melody, and as such, it is drawn out by the physical gesture.

MM   Right. The root of the word 'draw' is actually a Sanskrit word, "*dhrajti*," meaning "to sweep on." Of course, you don't play the piano with the fingers alone, but with the whole body. Wholeness sounds.

FP   Well, there are other things going on. Accompaniment? How does that relate to the line?

MM   As a pianist, you are both soloist and your own accompanist. And the relationship between the melody and the accompaniment is critical. It is so easy for an accompaniment to overwhelm the line. The way we usually deal with that is to talk about balance between melody and accompaniment, but that's a deceptive term because it implies that the melody and the accompaniment have equal standing. The usual difficulty is that the accompaniment swallows the line. The right resolution is to have the line swallow the accompaniment, not an even balance, but the right imbalance. That means that the melody, or the line, must sound like a solo voice. And it must have the color and character it has when it is self-contained and self-sustained.

FP   The color that it would have if it were self-sustained?

MM   Yes, a practical way of dealing with this is to play the line alone so that it is complete in itself, as if you were a cellist or violinist or singer. The line would have to be self-sufficient. It's difficult for students to realize this because they have the sense that the melody needs the support of the accompaniment, and that melody and accompaniment share and share alike. It's anything but that. Apparently, for the student and even for advanced pianists, it is difficult to realize how independent the line must be, and how important it is to preserve the sonority and color of a solo voice for the melody itself. When I say it should sound like a solo, I mean just that. As if it were sounding alone. You will want to suppress the accompaniment much more than you thought at first. It's not a simple ratio. That distance between melody and accompaniment allows the melody to sound and seem to have a beautiful color. It's curious that the melody, when it is properly balanced, doesn't sound like a nice balance; it sounds as if it were quite alone, but with a kind of aura that the right relationship allows.

FP   Mortimer, I think I've heard even "good pianists" playing so that the accompaniment swallowed up the line.

MM   That's very true. Bruno Walter, the conductor, in his book, *Of Music and Music Making*, makes a point of this, and in turn quotes Richard Wagner who said that his eyes were opened when he heard Beethoven conducted so that it was clear that you pursue the "Melos" or melody. And Walter makes the same case, relentlessly pursuing the line. In orchestral performance this may be harder to keep in mind than when playing the piano. It is not old-fashioned to emphasize the melody. Neither does a string quartet or the orchestra make all parts equal but, on the contrary, will also stress the main line. The principal melody should be self-sustaining.

FP   Sometimes there is more than one line, multiple voices.

MM   When there are several voices, they are less often of equal importance. Then you must determine the relative importance of all the voices and when the emphasis may shift.

FP   Even in the Bach two- and three-part inventions?

MM   Perhaps more evenly stressed, although the motif or subject is first in one voice and then another. They share, at moments, usually material developed from the main subject; they may, at a point, have equal say.

FP   Mort, I was thinking of the first movement of Beethoven's *Moonlight Sonata*. The theme is clearly high in the right hand, and there is another slower song being sung in the bass. But I've heard accomplished concert pianists play that movement so that both the treble line and the lesser bass line were obliterated by the repeating triplet throughout.

MM   Yes. The principal theme clearly begins with the dotted rhythm in the treble. And the bass figure persists through much of the movement. It should be the stronger part in the beginning. If you hear the triplet figure leading, you are in trouble. The bass line dominates at first, then it falls into second place when the repeated figure enters. Then the triplet figure will be in third place.

FP   Well, I can usually play the main line, and I can initially hear that "ground" theme in the left hand, but when the main line arrives in the right hand it is hard even to hear the tune that the left hand is playing.

MM   I think that the longer and better one listens, the better one hears secondary and even lesser voices. You must listen to all voices, but some will be well in the background. I should say that there are exceptions to the rule of one voice being pre-eminent and other voices subservient. I would think of Scarlatti. The voices are almost equal in importance. According to Ralph Kirkpatrick, his biographer, Scarlatti played a harpsichord with only one manual, in which case you can't subordinate one voice to another. And indeed it sounds better when you do not.

FP   One manual?

MM   One keyboard. He had only one keyboard. A harpsichord with two keyboards allows one voice to be softer than the other.

FP   Sometimes it's hard to find the line in a piece.

MM   Especially in contemporary pieces. In the wonderful Debussy prelude called *Fireworks*, there is almost *no* melodic line except for a few measures. It's all movement and color. Rhythm and color. And that's quite exceptional. And there are places in Brahms, in some of the piano pieces, where it seems as if the line is deliberately let go. It is a bit unusual, but it is much more true in contemporary music. The piece may be all about texture or color, and the idea of line has been abandoned. It is a completely different design.

FP   If one isn't playing such a piece, but picks up a score that one isn't familiar with, are there any written clues to identify the line?

MM   There may not be written clues. However, if you play the separate voices, there will be one that is most independent and carries the piece forward. But if you are playing a work that has only pattern and configuration and color to hold it together, there may be only momentary fragments of line. There is some contemporary music where the point is to deny old premises or presumptions about what music is about to the point that you have the piece, *Silence*, that denies line or tone, and pieces that use sounds to shock. That's another matter.

FP   Mort, I recall that you said that one never starts playing outside of time. Do you ever start without a line?

MM   Of course, there are many works that begin with accompaniment only. But the line was the first thing that I used to ask young people to play. We would begin with simple melodies. And as soon as you have three notes, you have a little shape. Years ago, I heard Ernest Bloch lecture at the University of California. He made this point in a talk to young people. He played one note on his viola and asked if that was music. And there was a big discussion and the students decided that wasn't music. Then he played two notes and there was a big discussion, and they said, "Yes, that was music." So even with two notes, there is a line. There has to be movement but two notes will do.

      And there is the unwritten line, the phrase that includes all other phrases. The most important phrase mark is the one that is never written, the one that includes the whole piece, starting before the beginning and going past the end. Whatever you are playing has to be included in a grand gesture that ties everything together.

FP   The phrase that goes from beginning to end and even a little past either end?

MM   You might imagine an overarching line that is linked to the image of time. Ultimately, everything will be tied together.

FP   Is there any particular physical action involved in playing the line, other than what would be involved in playing individual notes?

MM   Yes, indeed. The line, remember, is created with the motion of the whole arm with the forearm leading the fingers. You play the piano not with the fingers, but with the whole body. If the whole motion with which you move and conduct yourself at the piano is inhibited, everything becomes cramped or forced, both tone and time, as well as the movement for shaping the line. So it is absolutely critical that you move easily. But there is no end to relaxing, because our customary state of tension is what we imagine as being relaxed. For every instrumentalist, the goal of complete freedom is a never-ending pursuit. A pianist is never through seeing if he can be yet more relaxed. And that has to go beyond the mere physiological letting go. It is as if you would dissolve the hand, as if it is so free that there is no physical connection in the touch between key and body. It is very much a matter of thought and concentration and intent, so it becomes mindful. While you cannot play without using the whole body, it is as if you have got the physical action out of the way. Movement and gesture translate tone into a meaningful shape. Finally, it is as if thought becomes tone.

7

Tone and Color

The more the colors harmonize, the more the outline becomes precise ... when the color is at its richest, the form has reached plenitude.

~ Paul Cezanne

MM   The material with which you work is tone. There is an incredible variety of tone, a huge palette. As students we often deal only with loud and soft, and that is much too limiting. There are other ways of changing the tone. Tone can be bright or warm, dense or diffuse, loud or soft, short or long. A line may be taut or relaxed, an aspect of rhythm also affecting the tone. These are the main distinctions, but they are not usually taught.

FP   How does one create tone of these differing types?

MM   Well, loud and soft are usually understood to be created by the rapidity of the travel of the key.

FP   Not the force? The speed?

MM   I'm not certain you can distinguish between force and speed. It ends up being the speed with which the hammer travels. Some say it is wrong to work with color as a reality since tone color changes with loudness. But they lose the point when they say that quality varies only as does loudness. Why think only loud or soft when what may concern us is tone quality?

FP   OK, then how does one distinguish between bright and warm?

MM   A key that is started briskly, an initial swift motion, produces a bright tone. A warm tone is obtained by moving the key as slowly as possible at first, commensurate with the needed loudness.

FP   So, if you wanted a warm, loud tone, you'd have to depress the key slowly at first and then rapidly?

MM   Absolutely.

FP   And that would differ from rapidly at first, and then slowly, which would lead to a bright, soft tone.

MM   I think that's what happens. And, in fact, if you want to play loudly without harshness, you need to get a tone that is yet warmer because it will otherwise be unacceptably harsh.

FP   I, myself, have no awareness of the speed of my key depression at each stage.

MM   Well, I don't think you can. You might want to know about it, but you can hardly deal with it in a mechanical way. Actually, you have to listen to the tone and just realize the mechanics involved. You have to know what you want and what the difference is between a warm tone and a bright one. Imagine playing Scarlatti in a style of Brahms; it would sound dreadful. The Scarlatti line is very thin and bright and the Brahms line very warm and full.

FP   The way this tangles me up is that I can visualize the difference between a bright painting and a warm one, but I'm less sure about sounds and even less so about how to make them as a pianist.

MM   Perhaps it would help to know that the most important thing is to think the sound that you want. Try to hear it. Even though we've been discussing the mechanics, what matters most is having an image of the sound you want to produce.

FP   OK. What about the distinction between a dense tone and a diffuse one?

MM   A dense tone is obtained by thinking to produce the sound near the bottom of the key dip. You can get a tone at the piano by moving the key less than a quarter of the way down. You can start anywhere in the depression of the key. The question is, where is the tone? You have to aim to the point in the dip of the key where you hear the hit. Matthay terms this the "time spot."

FP   Well then, it seems that it would be easy to produce a tone that would be loud and dense, because it would require a fast descent of the key to get the sound near the bottom. And easy to have a soft, diffuse, warm sound.

MM   That's true. The dynamic levels tend to go in one direction or another. But that's why it is important for the pianist to realize that they are separate qualities. Not just loud and soft. These things don't matter at all if they aren't handled consistently. It is only when these differences become clear to the pianist, and when they are handled consistently that they become part of the tonal palette.

FP   Hmm. Short and long sounds easy.

MM   Well, actually it is not. Some pianists seem to know only two lengths, *legato* and *staccato*. And they play *staccato* as short as possible, as if there was nothing between. Music dictionaries are vague when defining the length of a *staccato* note, perhaps intentionally so. You can easily distinguish seven lengths from the longest to the shortest tone. First, *legattissimo*, where tones overlap, then *legato*, one note connected to the next. Then, *portamento*, indicated by a *staccato* note under a slur, just barely separate. To demonstrate, play the scale with one finger, connecting it as well as you can. There will be a small break as if you had carried one tone to the other. Next, a note may be marked by a wedge, and is about 2/3 the length of the printed tone. The wedge was regarded by Couperin as an ornament, and was called *"l'aspiration."*

It is as if you shortened the note to take a breath. It is indicated by a pointed dash. This usage seems consistent from Haydn to Schubert. Then comes *staccato*. I think that you should assume it is half the printed note and then modify it as seems appropriate. Next is *staccatissimo*, which is a very short *staccato*. With the hand still on or near the keys, you can release the note before half its time has gone by, except in the fastest tempo when it is not possible to make such fine distinctions. At the fastest tempo even *staccato* will turn into something like *portamento*. And the last is *marcattissimo*, my own term. It is a note that can be made shorter yet by playing the note *forte*, pulling the finger off the front of the keys. And *forte* because the key must rebound and the damper cut the note off more quickly.

FP   So there is more to short and long than I thought.

MM   More than most pianists think. And puzzling, since this is all very measurable and the distinctions can be easily made, once discovered. It allows one to be more consistent. And all of these touches have their uses. Of course, loud and soft have all the gradations from fortissimo to pianissimo, but students are seldom asked to play all these levels. It isn't difficult to get something in between mezzopiano and mezzoforte, or between mezzoforte and forte. That too increases the variety of the tonal palette.

FP   Sometimes it seems to me that you can substitute one quality for another. Some places ask for a *crescendo,* and I find speeding up or slowing a bit provides the same effect as a *crescendo*. It increases tension that somehow seems to replace the increased volume.

MM   I'm not sure it replaces it since the effect is different. I think it is very important to distinguish between these qualities.

FP   But I'm not sure all those combinations are really available. For example, it seems to get harder and harder to play something loud that is also diffuse.

MM   That's true. Not all these combinations are equally accessible. To get away from too mechanical an approach, I should say that a tone can meet several of these requirements and be perfectly appropriate, but not be spiritual enough. A tone produced mechanically sounds mechanical. A tone must be a spiritual tone, that is to say, alive. It is necessary to get well past dealing with that button, the piano key. Cultivate the ability to let it happen. Then it seems to come out of relaxation and intention, and not mechanics. I was re-reading the passage which I like so much in *The Art of Archery* where the master archer says, "You are innocent of that right shot." And the key word used was "innocent." That's the point; it has to be out of innocence. You can't do it out of knowledge. If you calculate it all, it won't work. Especially if you know a lot.

FP   Is this then one of those activities where you are best off if you do a huge preparation, and then throw away all your notes and just do the performance?

MM   It's so. Everything is preparation.

FP   You know Musashi's *Five Rings of Power?* He was
an accomplished samurai warrior who then retired to a
cave to contemplate life, and to write a manual for samurai. Some contemporary Japanese corporations use it in
training their executives. I recall his prescribing a great
deal of spiritual preparation then finally exhorting the
warrior to just go out and cut the other fellow. The faster
and the quicker the better. That seemed to me a sort of
joke, but now, as I think about it, perhaps he was saying
that once you have established the right frame of mind,
you had to let loose of all of the specifics and just do the
act.

MM   It sounds like what we've been discussing.

8

The Musical Line and Style

Thus style forms itself out of feeling when led by taste.
~ Ferrucio Busoni

FP   What about style?

MM   All composers have their unique style which is manifest in the quality of the line. Four characteristic elements determine this, three of tone and one of time. Characteristics of tone are brightness, thickness, and density, while the line is distinguished by its degree of tension.

FP   Yes, we've discussed those parameters. Are there any other important ones?

MM   I think those are the most useful ones. There are others; for example, the amount of pedal that one would use. This affects the line, but I regard that as a secondary quality, except for Debussy where it is of equal importance.

FP   Would you consider Mozart for a minute? Would you think it right to consider the line in terms of humor, such as tongue in cheek, or perhaps an occasional wink?

MM   It is clear that Mozart often may express prankish and even boisterous humor. I think that is outside of the characteristics of the line itself; that has to do with the kind of expression we may intend and create with the particular line. If you played Mozart with a rather thick and dense line, as in Bartok or Beethoven, you would preclude an expression that is central to Mozart. So expression is all-important and finally determining, but it's only one of the objective elements affecting style.

FP   So style has to do with the quality of the line and the expression.

MM   That's a nice way of putting it. I like that.

FP   Well, if we go back then, perhaps we can talk about those characteristics of the line some more. For example, bright or warm? I still find it easier to see the visual equivalent than to understand exactly what that means musically.

MM   I don't feel qualified to discuss color in painting, but I would say bright in painting is quite likely an equivalent of a bright tone, a tone that emphasizes the higher partials, and at the piano, a tone that is produced with a very quick motion of the key. A tone of equal loudness produced with an initial slow movement of the key is perceived as warm.

FP   This deals with an individual note then. A single note is perceived as being bright or warm.

MM   I would say, yes. However, it is easier to recognize a tone as bright when it is in the company of other bright notes.

FP   And you also said that dense or diffuse has to do with tone color.

MM   Yes. If you produce a tone near the bottom of the key dip, it will have a different quality from the tone that is produced with a shallow touch. The shallow touch, or diffuse line, is equivalent to a visual line that is painted with a rather watery brush.

FP   Let me see if I understand this. The shallow touch? You have to push the key down far enough to throw the hammer up to hit the string.

MM   That's absolutely right. And as pianists, this point is never made clear to us, but on any good piano you can move the key abruptly one quarter of the way down or less, and the hammer will strike the string. You can start at that point and go another quarter of the way down, and you will get a tone again. And you can start the key half the way down and get a tone. You can't start at the very bottom. You get no tone at all, or, for your effort, a very small tone. And I've discovered that depth of touch is almost always an instinctive matter, so that even the most awkward student can hear and copy without further explanation.

FP   Do I understand you to mean that when the intended tone is near the end of the dip of the key, that's likely to produce a dense line?

MM   Yes. The visual equivalent is a very black line. A dark line.

FP   What does that have to do with loud or soft?

MM   It is a separate quality that can be perceived as distinct from loud or soft. If you are playing very loudly, it is often the case that it may be a denser tone. But, in fact, even the loudest tone is not produced by aiming at the very bottom of the dip.

FP   So it is possible, at least theoretically, to have a loud tone, producing a wide line, that would not be a dense tone.

MM   That's true, as in Debussy, usually, but I would grant that at the extreme of a soft range it would be difficult to produce a very dense line. And, at the very loudest, it might be difficult to produce a tone that seemed diffuse. We can limit our description of the line to these four features. That will serve for most styles.

FP   All right. Considering just bright-warm and dense-diffuse, distinctions that have to do with a quick or slower key movement and the depth of touch, what if we just spoke in those terms? Instead of saying it was a bright, dense piece, we said that it was a piece in which the keys were depressed quickly to the bottom?

MM   I would be very uncomfortable with that because what we want to deal with is the effect, and when you become involved with the *how*, you are in trouble. If I begin to analyze how I walk, I will probably end up kicking the tea table and spilling things. This mechanical analysis may be helpful for some, but for most pianists it is better to concentrate on the quality of the sound desired.

FP   Well, I'm glad to hear that. I don't think I could remember all these mechanical techniques anyway. How about the taut-relaxed business? You said that is a rhythmic phenomenon, by which I assume you couldn't define it by one note, but rather a sequence of notes in time.

MM   Yes, it has to do with the movement through time. You might understand this by drawing your arm through the air, so that you feel that it is really pulling, instead of drawing the hand through the air without energy. And the same thing applies to the production of a musical line at the piano. If I'm phrasing, and the whole arm is slack and doesn't represent the musical gesture, it will lack energy. Relaxed, but without sufficient tension.

FP   Are there pieces that are relaxed and without energy?

MM   I think you could find moments in works where that would be true. I hesitate to say that there is anything that you don't do some of the time. But I think that would be the exception.

FP   So it sounds like most pieces or lines have some degree of tautness.

MM   Yes, but remember that the tension in the line is only one expression of energy in the line. The character of the tone itself can also express energy. Tension in the line is a very important expression of energy, especially musical energy. One has, in each style, to find the musical outlet for energy. For example, in Haydn, a very taut line, the energy is overtly rhythmic, while the energy in a more relaxed Mozart line is lyric or singing. To play the Mozart with more energy you would have to find an appropriate lyric expression.

FP   Going on to the wide and thin. Roughly equivalent to loud and soft?

MM   I think that is right.

FP   There are loud and soft notes?

MM   Well, within any style. But I think that the outer limit in each style will generally be perceived as the width of the line itself. If I'm to play very *forte* in the Mozart, there will be a definite limit, and it can't go to the Beethoven *forte*. If I'm going to play, perhaps near the outer limit of loudness, a Scarlatti *forte* is not going to reach the level of a forte in Brahms. The Brahms is a bigger tone, of course.

FP   So the Scarlatti line is thinner because its loud notes are not as loud as they are in a thick line?

MM   Right. And softer dynamics, relatively softer, of course.

FP   It's puzzling to me to hear you describe characteristics of individual notes that somehow produce an overall character of an entire line. To go back to the mechanical description of a piece that's loud, and involves notes hit quickly and descending fully, we end up with a bright, dense, wide line.

MM   Well, Bartok is the closest. A Bartok line is one that is past the middle in brightness; it's a very dense line and a very wide one, so that a Bartok *forte* is really generous, but it isn't all that warm. It's incisive, and the rhythmic element is very important too. With all that, you have described a Bartok line.

FP   Quite taut?

MM   I'm thinking of the Bartok sonata and lots of the pieces in *Microkosmos* — not very taut, sort of in the middle. A Scarlatti line is much more taut. A Debussy line is more relaxed and diffuse.

FP   If these are the characteristics of the line itself, and the styles of the individual composers can be described in terms of these characteristics of the line, perhaps you can describe some of the composers I'm more familiar with. What if we start with Chopin? Is that fair? Is he really the sort of composer one can talk about this way?

MM   Above all. He's the pianist's composer. I have a good image for the Chopin line, and one that reflects the qualities we've been talking about. It is an unusual photo of a model of Chopin's hand. It has the look of immense fluidity, grace, and refinement. His would be a line that is not too taut, a color that is a little bit on the sweet side, perhaps a better word, on the warm side, where the energy is lyric and expressed as singing, where tautness, rhythmic tautness, is not overt, except for the mazurkas, but the energy is manifest as singing or lyric . . . intense, fluid. As to warm and bright, it is on the warm side. It is not a very dense line, nor very heavy or wide.

FP   The description of Chopin sounds like a reasonably good, but not very tasty, dish. It's not very bright, not too dense, halfway between taut and relaxed, and halfway between thin and thick. Not outstanding in any way.

MM   I would just have to say this isn't a spice cabinet, and we're not getting what is tasty by exploiting the extremes. We're getting at what is characteristic. There is a very special, intense, lyric color that you want, a uniquely vocal line above all, that I regard as very characteristic and something to strive for in Chopin.

FP   When I play Chopin, and say, "What wonderful, beautiful melodies," am I talking about a vocal line? The melodies all sound singable.

MM   Yes. When I say vocal, I mean the normal tensions in the human voice. We want the piano to sound like a voice with the special character appropriate for Chopin.

It was Casals who told his orchestra, when he conducted in Barcelona, that the highest goal was to "make the music speak." That was a personal goal of mine, so I was pleased to read Casal's comment.

FP   When music speaks, it sings.

MM   And when music sings, it speaks.

FP   All right, so that is Chopin. Relaxed, warm, an enormous lyric energy, slightly diffuse, and not very thin. How about Beethoven?

MM   A very characteristic line that is dense and fairly wide. Not as dense as Bartok, but a very substantial tone that is obtained with a deep touch and sufficient weight.

FP   What about the degree of brightness?

MM   I think a Beethoven line is usually not too bright. Although you will find the instruction "*e con brio*," and that means with brightness, nevertheless, I think a Beethoven line will be slanted toward the warm side. Not lush, not overripe, but a warm color.

FP   Taut? Relaxed?

MM   In the middle. Not wholly or overtly motivated by rhythm alone. And not as relaxed as a Schumann line may seem to be, or a Debussy line.

FP   Is Beethoven almost always like this? Are there

any Beethoven pieces that are radically different?

MM   I think perhaps some of the bagatelles in *Opus 119*. It's dangerous to have too obvious a solution; nevertheless, they can be helpful and clarify differences. I think you can find exceptions, and you can find an early period in Beethoven on the bright side, those sonatas dedicated to Haydn, but it's already a marked departure in weight, width and warmth.

FP   How about Mozart?

MM   With regard to warm and bright, I like the term *dolce* for Mozart, which is of course on the warm side, but perhaps sweet rather than warm, since with warm I usually associate a wider line. I like *dolce*.

FP   If warmth has to do with speed of movement of the key initially, what is sweet?

MM   Less broad, yet warm. After all, *dolce* is a common instruction. Intent is important. You intend a tone that is sweet, not abrupt, not harsh, but gentle. Intent is everything As for density, the dense line or dark color is not appropriate. Mozart's ethereal quality is gained with a lighter brush.

FP   If I just think about the melody of a Mozart piece, I find "diffuse" a distressing term to use. It sounds imprecise.

MM   There's nothing imprecise about a light line. It is focused; it is lyric; it is singing; and, it is not dense.

Mozart is sometimes played as if it is all things neat, precise, dry and clean, but I think that's not what Mozart is about.

FP   I think that I've heard Mozart played sometimes in a very mechanical way. Will we get to that in discussing the time and rhythmic features?

MM   I'm sure that Mozart never intended his music to sound mechanical. However, there is a moment in a late C major Haydn sonata in which he imitates a music box. And I think it right to play that in a mechanical way. But really this is an exception.

FP   Then let's ask about the character of the Mozart line in terms of the taut-relaxed spectrum.

MM   Let us say that the Mozart line moves away from taut, past the middle toward relaxed, the energy not being overtly rhythmic, but lyrical, manifest as singing.

FP   The width? Mozart would probably not be as wide as Beethoven.

MM   Not as wide as Beethoven, and not even so wide as Chopin. Softer. On a scale of ten, Mozart would never reach past seven, and as soft as you please, although in my recollection, Mozart never uses any thing softer than pianissimo. Bartok, for example, uses four pianos and even five, followed by the term 'estinto.'

FP   I'm not sure I fully understand this yet. Perhaps

you've already answered this. What would be wrong to simply say that a Mozart line is softer as opposed to saying it is thinner?

MM   Nothing would be wrong. Softer is the auditory image; thinner is the visual image. We're talking about the degree of loudness that is constant through the dynamic range for that composer. If a composer is consistent in the entire range, then it becomes an element of the style. Some of these distinctions are almost immeasurable but in context are very apparent. They matter only to the degree that the pianist is aware and consistent.

FP   Let me summarize some of what you just said. It is getting into my dense, but not soft head. A given note in Mozart might be louder or softer than a given note in Beethoven, but on the whole, it doesn't contain quite the width, that is, the loudness of Beethoven. Does it not contain the extremes of softness too? Does the width of the line have anything to do with the extremes of softness?

MM   Usually not. It is the relative value and character of all the notes in a line — and the sentiment expressed — that will determine the style.

FP   As an aside, can you think of a composer whose line is both bright and dense?

MM   Prokofiev.

FP   Prokofiev. That reminds me. I have been working

on a Schubert *Impromptu*, the first in *Opus 90*.

MM   Yes? A very nice piece. It starts with a chord in the full orchestra.

FP   Full orchestra, did you say?

MM   Yes. If you orchestrated it, the chord wouldn't be in the violins alone. It would be in the full orchestra. It helps to consider how the piece would be played by an orchestra. Especially with this piece, where so much that happens is the same idea with a different setting. Then you start with an empty space. If you start with the empty space, it will go better.

FP   Well, Mort, the really puzzling part, and the reason I am asking about it right now, is that there is a very exciting part, about measure 140, where there are powerful chords in the right hand that accompany the melody in octaves in the left hand. I find it very like Prokofiev.

MM   Aha! Well, maybe you are playing the Schubert much like Prokofiev. I have a story to tell you. Prokofiev does have a steely, biting character. Bernhard Abramowitsch loved Schubert and was a Schubert specialist. Abramowitsch was playing a Prokofiev sonata in Prokofiev's presence when Prokofiev stopped him and said, "Perhaps you could play it a little more like Schubert." Amusing in that circumstance, but I've always felt Prokofiev was a lyrical sheep in dissonant wolve's clothing. So maybe you are right. Perhaps you are overemphasizing the chords. The line is pre-eminent.

The chords must be played very calmly, not overexcitedly, keeping the flow. The line is still primary. The difficulty and the flamboyance of the chords draws your attention to them. You have to play them from the surface, very relaxedly.

FP   OK, that helps clarify the style question. What of another composer? What about Scarlatti?

MM   A line that is bright and pulled more taut than any other. Stretched almost to the breaking point.

FP   Any other composers whose lines are as taut as Scarlatti's?

MM   Ravel comes to mind, an impressionist. Both style and expression are utterly different from Scarlatti, but the line is very taut and thin, perhaps even more intense.

FP   Help me understand taut again. Do I understand a line that is taut obliges the notes to come precisely at the right moment? No slackness about where to put those notes?

MM   Yes, but that answer must be modified, because in any style, the notes must come at the right time interval. It is partly a matter of gesture. You mean to draw a line that is truly pulling. The line expresses great tension.

FP   This reminds me of instructions I found on the piano one day 30 years ago, when you had gone out and I had arrived for a lesson. They said something like "sit in a totally relaxed position and maintain great tension in the line, yet play with infinite flexibility."

MM   A remark I likely made. Contradiction is at the root of all things.

FP   Before we talk about expression, do we have unfinished business about the quality of the line?

MM   No. We could go on and define every composer in terms of the qualities of the line. But I think we've outlined the approach.

FP   Well, let's talk about expression. Does that word sound right? Something more than the quality of the line? Imposed upon the line by the pianist? By the composer?

MM   Probably an interaction between music, composer, and pianist. However, the expression comes out of the musical design and is never imposed from without. In music, and I dare say any work of art, it is the suitable match of form and expression that makes it strong. Expression is the shape, and the shape is the expression. Expression isn't anything you put in or put on. It has to come out of your immediate perception of the shape, the musical shape. And the line creates the shape. There's a rather primitive analogy to those puzzles with dots and numbers where there is not a shape until you literally draw a line between numbers. At the piano you draw a line between tones to perceive the musical shape. The piano playing that is antimusical, unmusical, is found in performances where notes are isolated.

FP   I'm still not sure what expression is. I think I understand what the line is, and the line creates the shape for the music. The line is the most important element.

MM   Remember that line, although important, is not the only means of expression. Rhythm, movement, harmonic color, without line, can create an expressive design. Expression could be defined as the feeling that arises on perceiving the musical idea. There is the remark of Beethoven in the margin of one of his quartets: "From the heart to the heart."

FP   Expression is the composer's emotion transmitted through the performer to the listener.

MM   Yes. Remember, expression is not measurable and not precise, and that's part of music's charm and its impact. Expression is a matter of feeling.

FP   How does one find expression in a line other than through the characteristics of a line that we've already dealt with?

MM   This is another level of magic. But I believe that anyone who can hear high or low, as a gesture, will feel that it is an expression, albeit a musical one, and that it expresses feeling. In the end, music is the communication of feeling. If one does not perceive it as gesture, as tone and as movement, how can it be expressive?

FP   It seems that we are just beginning to touch on

the really important issues, like what music is really about. Can you say that explicitly?

MM   "No" would be the prudent answer. I think it was Mendelssohn who said that the expression in music was too precise to be expressed in words! But I think music is about expressing feelings, and creating designs that are expressive of feelings with tone. Music is a design out of tone, rooted in dancing and singing. Design, not only in the sense of pattern, but also meaning intention, usually with emotional significance. Ultimately, structure creates meaning, and meaning, in turn, generates structure. Is that an answer to the question, or is it more like a long evasion?

FP   Yes!

9

Energy and Expression

Energy: strength of expression, force of utterance, life, spirit.
~ *Webster's New International Dictionary, Unabridged*

MM   Energy has many manifestations. It can be energy
with which you produce a tone, it can be the strength of
expression; it can be aliveness, the spiritual quality in the
tone. Energy can be manifest as loudness, as clarity. All of
those have to do with strength of expression. I like the
word "energy" rather than "expression" because "expression" may have a tendency to encourage emoting and
exaggeration.

FP   What does that have to do with playing the piano?

MM   Everything. The strongest playing is the most
expressive, so energy is central to our task. To play with
the greatest energy you must be equally relaxed. Then
you won't block yourself and the expression will be direct
and honest. A direct response releases emotional energy.

FP   This is bewildering. How does one play with great energy and stay equally relaxed? Is that possible?

MM   That's not only possible, but it's necessary. When working to develop a more adequate technique, I had set a simple-seeming goal, to play with the greatest possible energy. I would come to a point, short of the goal, when only relaxing yet more would allow me to go further. Finally, I found that to play with all my might I had to relax totally. That was an absolute contradiction.

FP   So you were not trying to play with great loudness, but great energy.

MM   Yes. A *forte* is a particular, but not the only expression of energy. It became clear that one can play *piano* or *forte* with equal energy.

FP   How does one do that? Play softly or loudly with equal energy.

MM   It has to do with focus, with acuteness, with response and awareness. One discovers that it is possible to play softly and not lose intensity. Actors do that on the stage using a stage whisper. You speak softly with all of your might. It is the same at the piano. You play softly with all of your might. That becomes not physical or mechanical, but rather spiritual, which is to say more alive.

FP   If you wanted a student to play softly with all of his might, play spiritually, what would you say if he were having trouble.

MM   If a student couldn't grasp this, I'd use the the-
atrical analogy and suggest speaking quietly with a great
deal of energy. Or ask the student to play *fortissimo* and
then repeat the passage *pianissimo* with as much energy.
A young student quite able to play softly with energy said
it was "sweet energy." A nice image.

FP   Can you tell the difference between someone
playing softly and slowly with great energy, and someone
playing softly and slowly with little energy?

MM   Oh, I could demonstrate it very easily. You could
do it too.

FP   Where do you feel the energy? Not kinetic.

MM   You hear it. It is manifest as a tone exactly intended. And it is manifest as a different color, and as easiness.
It must feel easy.

FP   OK, perfect Mortimer Markoff. We're now playing
with great energy, neither fast nor loud, and playing easily.

MM   You might call it "Mortimer Markoff," but it is
obvious that it is exactly parallel to the bow and arrow
discussion in Herrigel's *Zen and The Art of Archery*. It is
what I am taught in my Tai Chi class. Chi is, by definition,
spiritual energy. In Sumo wrestling, after the ceremonial
bows, one sometimes simply acknowledges that the
other has won. They don't need the physical confronta-
tion. They have felt the spiritual energy and known who
would win.

FP   Oh me. Let me understand, are you always playing with great spiritual energy?

MM   Yes, I think that energy is a constant. Strength of expression is a constant. Even when the music implies abnegation or resignation.

FP   Mort, when you are playing with what I would recognize as more physical energy, faster or louder or both, does that do anything to the spiritual energy? Is it lessened?

MM   I think that can happen, but it's not what you'd like. *Forte* playing can be either spiritual or physical. And you want the former, not the latter. I want to emphasize that the energy used is spiritual energy, and the tone will reflect it. However, if a tone denies time or motion, it won't be appropriate tone. When teaching, I would speak of motion, then walk away from the piano as the student began. Sometimes I would say "right" after the first tone and indeed it would be right. And I thought how fine that I could distinguish from one tone whether or not it would be moving. Later I thought to ask students the same question and discovered that any attentive student could tell as well as I. You need only to ask the question. The important thing is that tone itself is an expression of time so it's not really possible to separate these two.

FP   Tone itself is an expression of time.

MM   Can be! An expression of time.

FP   This is getting more and more metaphysical. Are we dealing in magic?

MM   Believe me, it is magic, as with many things we take for granted, life for instance. There are those musicians who say you can't affect tone quality, only loudness, whether it's a finger or a pencil or a broomstick. And yet, they will say that the piano can be cheerful or sorrowful, noble or abject, whatever you like. It has all kinds of meaning that this poor box, the piano, never heard about. But I don't want to digress....

FP   Why not? And, if we can digress, I'd say that I don't think of my piano as a box. In fact, I always assume that my piano has a soul.

MM   That's an assumption I'd never quarrel with. Most pianists become quite attached to, even in love with, their pianos.

FP   This sense of moving — you say that one tone can tell you whether the piece is moving. What exactly is moving?

MM   First, the expression of time's flow, that is, duration. Second, the tone reflects a musically expressive gesture. The language isn't coincidental. When we say that something is moving, we mean both, it is expressive and it expresses motion. The very word "emotion" is simply "motion" with "e" before it.

FP   Well then, whatever this concept of energy is, it is

something that should be maintained throughout the piece, without which the piece is not as good, and it is not equivalent to how loud or fast you are playing. Does it have to do with the tension of the line?

MM   It has a lot to do with that.

FP   Now suppose you had someone who was playing in a less energetic fashion, expression lacking, how do you move them up to a more energetic level?

MM   Well, first I play the same passage, as well as I can with and again without energy, so that they hear that difference. You can do the same thing with the voice. If I speak with little or no energy, it will seem to lack definition and fail to carry. It is a matter of definition and projection.

    Joseph Hoffman said it very well: "As to theory, 'great energy, great results.' I prefer my emendation: Great energy, restrained power, and moderate manifestation of it. Prepare the finger for great force, imagine the tone as being strong, and yet strike moderately." Long before I was in a Tai Chi class and could see the parallels, I noted that to provide more energy, you must relax. Relaxing, or letting go, and developing more energy are complementary.

FP   What more is there to say about energy?

MM   Realize that energy must be kept in reserve. Think about a pipe organ. The energy is literally equivalent to the amount of air stored in the bellows. If it is all expended, there is nothing left and the instrument won't speak. It is stored energy that is necessary for a very strong performance, and that speaks of restraint. At the piano, energy seems to be stored by waiting in the silent time space. So energy has a lot to do with duration and, incidentally, with right breathing.

FP   OK, I'm beginning to understand that this sense of rhythm does pervade all understanding of what happens in the music.

MM   Yes. The energy is in the field. The time field and the silent space. The negative.

FP   Oh yes, you talked about the negative and called it the ground. You included the silence, calm, the opposite of all the active things we usually talk about. Now you are saying that the energy is in those?

MM   Yes. Equally. On both sides of the balance. Energy is a constant, not only at the beginning of a tone, but in its duration and in the silence. Energy is constant in tension and in letting go. In expression and in repose or calm, in expending energy and in conserving it. To play with your entire strength, you must save all your energy at the same time.

FP   Mort, I'm going to go down and stare at the piano. And when I'm done staring at it, I will say, "That was really well played, perhaps the best I've ever done." I think I will stare my way through some very difficult piece I've never been able to master, perhaps the *Appassionata*.

MM   Good. That should do it.

10

Technique

Generally speaking, abandonment and suppleness are Liszt's mottos... He does not approve of giving a meticulous finish to the compositions for he wants their spirit understood... As for finger technique, he never wants striking on the extremity of the finger or the nail, but instead on the ball of the finger, which flattens the finger, of course, and allows it freedom.
~ The Liszt Pedagogue, Madame Auguste Boissier

FP   What do you mean by piano technique?

MM   I mean a technique that will allow you to play musically and not mechanically. Ordinarily we mean playing the right notes at the right time and with the right dynamics. That is a rather primitive definition. The result will be unmusical. We need to distinguish between piano technique in the usual sense and a technique for musical performance. To be concerned with mechanical perfection only works all too well; the result is playing that is perfectly mechanical. You will create an inevitable split between music and technique unless technique is practiced *musically*. Even at a high level you can distinguish between those pianists who are concerned with piano playing and those concerned with making music.

FP   This is a little too metaphysical for me. What do you do? How do you make that distinction work?

MM   By making your musical goals very clear and never practicing technical patterns mechanically. Give studies the attention you would give to a musical composition. To cultivate a musical technique, establish a rhythm governed by flow, albeit measured by the beat, and listen with the closest attention to the tone, especially to the beginning of each tone. It means associating tone, touch, and the key and above all, listening so that the smallest shape is played mindfully, never automatically or mechanically. It means listening for the line and recognizing how the movement of the entire arm, wrist and hand creates the line.

FP   This sounds like the same old story. I don't understand what you have said new about technique.

MM   All right then. What if I say that the most important premise for all technique is relaxedness. Since you play the piano by moving, any tension that impedes movement is a handicap. Remaining relaxed, in order to allow the most pliant easy motion, is the necessary condition for musicality to be manifest. Remember Chopin's statement, *"Souplesse est toute"*... flexibility or suppleness is everything.

FP   OK Now it sounds like we are getting to something I can identify as a technical phenomenon. How relaxed do you want me? Totally paralyzed?

MM   On the contrary, total tension means paralysis. If relaxed, you move easily. If you were seated at the piano and totally relaxed, you'd fall off the piano bench, right? On the other hand, if you remain seated easily and are comfortable yet relaxed, you would know you are only using those muscles that are necessary. By extension, that applies to any action that follows. If I raise my arm and it seems to me that it is easy, relaxed, and without effort, you will say that there are some muscles that are working but we are not thinking of those. You are thinking of the right action and concentrating on doing nothing else. We call people who act without resistance, naturals. Naturals aren't very common. I sometimes think we should call them unnaturals! Most of us take our cues for any activity from the resistance we find in doing it, whether swinging a bat or playing tennis or whatever. A natural takes cues from what feels easy. And when they do something and feel no resistance at all they are quite happy. Whereas we more common unnaturals believe such phrases as "try harder." What we have to do, of course, is "try easier." Which is to not take cues from muscle groups that offer resistance to any desired action.

FP   I'm a little puzzled. I'm not quite sure whether you are describing what one does or how it looks after one has done it.

MM   I'm describing what one does *not* do. And when it looks right, it doesn't look like anything. I used to have a little catechism, "When you play a single tone and it is right, what do you do?" The answer should be "Nothing." "And what does it feel like?" "Nothing." And what does it look like?" The answer should be, "It looks perfectly natural and easy."

FP   Wait a minute. You do something. You depress the key.

MM   Yes, you do. But understand, this is a way of saying, "Do the very least." What happens when you reach out and pick up a cup, a customary and easy action? You don't think of really doing anything, you just do it. If I think of how I do it, I'm already in trouble. If I analyze the movements involved in doing it, I'm in deeper trouble. And if I figured it out exactly, then it will be difficult indeed. But I agree, when we must analyze an activity, we may have to go through those steps. Much of a right action has to do with thought, and then the physical part resulting naturally.

FP   OK. But I do hear you describing these phenomena mostly as what they are not. If so, tell me again, precisely, just what good technique is not doing.

MM   You are not tightening, guiding, forcing, or consciously doing. Nor are you holding the hand in a fixed position or playing on the tips of the fingers, which Liszt detested, nor are you striking from above the key but making contact with the ball or fleshy part of the fingers. Although you are thinking the music intently, physically you are letting it be and letting yourself be. If you have students who are rigid and mannered, where nothing happens freely, then you have to go back to the other extreme and figure out how it is you do the least.

FP   And how is that?

MM   Here we're back to the other extreme, the detail.
For a single tone, you can analyze what the conditions
are. For the whole body, it is to be tall without rigidity,
half on the bench, the back straight, slightly slanted
forward. The forearm level, the fingers — and here it
departs from what is conventional — the fingers in that
unheld position, in the loose curve they fall in when the
arm drops to the side. You bring the arm up without any
effort at all, the elbows slightly out, and place the fingers
on the keys and they are almost flat, resting on the
padded part of the finger, not on the tip. When you
want to sound a single tone, you do the least you can.
Touching the key, before you play it, your action is a little
like clasping, but in no way like hitting. You allow the arm
to float. Suspended. As if the arm was weightless. That is
the condition of the whole apparatus, a condition of
doing nothing, just being suspended and buoyant.

   Then you have to deal with the key, which is really a recalcitrant device for producing the tone. You have
to depress the key, but it is well to know something we
are seldom taught —- that the tone can be produced
near the first, the middle, or the last part of the dip. So,
using that English teacher Matthay's term, you have to
aim the key to a *time spot*, what you might call a *tone
spot*, where the tone begins. So, you have to be very
sensitive to the key and to touch.

   Total relaxedness is the only way you can be
aware of the resistance that the key makes. It's a little like
weighing an envelope in your hand. No one has to tell
you that your arm has to be held very lightly or you won't

feel anything at all. And the reverse, as if you were weighing the key that is resisting upwards instead of down. So that has to do with the key and the arm and the whole stance of the person at the keyboard.

But there is more to it than that. It's wrong to presume that it is easy to listen to a piano tone. It starts with a noise although we're wanting to hear a beautiful tone. That begins a split second after the thump or the "hit", as I call it. Learn to listen to the hit as part of the tone.

FP   I don't understand why listening to the hit, something quite distinct from the following tone, adds anything to my awareness or my ability to play well.

MM   Well, listening acutely is the whole point.

FP   But, why must I listen so acutely to something that has little to do with the music?

MM   It has everything to do with music. That's your material. You can't control it unless you listen for it. It's a nuisance. The ear tends to reject the abrupt beginning of the tone. And it changes perception to listen to the hit. Since timing is critical, you have no acute control unless you listen acutely. Such a right tone I call an "honest tone"; you are well aware of the hit, very conscious of the touch, and very relaxed. These three, being relaxed, listening, and touching, allow you to focus on the detail, a single tone. And the problem is great because you cannot hold the material in your hand. No matter what instrument you play, flute or violin, guitar or voice. You make the connection by *associating* tone, touch, and time. And finally, the place where the key is at the instant the tone begins. And that association must be very close. It may seem, in a lucky moment, as if you are touching the tone. It will seem to you as if time, tone and touch match, an illusion, but a wonderful one. As if you are touching the tone. And the language reflects that. We say "that person has a nice touch." That closeness, that immediacy, that transfer of energy that is exact, has a great effect. You feel that connection, and the listener does too. And that is the function of touch. The piano and the pianist are one.

FP   You know, we may continue with all these conversations and never get to what I thought was playing the piano. It all seems to have to do with getting ready for things. Preparation. Everything is preface.

MM   Well, we start playing the piano by focusing on a single tone. That can be practiced with Hanon exercises or scales or whatever you are playing. Be forewarned. Concern with detail alone is a terrible trap; you may lose sight of the whole shape. The next level has to do with playing more than single tones but combining them to get the line. That involves the whole motion of the arm, an essential part of good technique. The whole arm must move in advance of the fingers so as to draw the line. And if the motion is inhibited or cramped or in any way impeded, that will leave you with a lot of notes but not very much music.

FP   A clutter of notes.

MM   A clutter of notes.

FP   But no line?

MM   You won't be drawing the shape, the phrase. And I could include as part of the technique the ability to sound tones in the right rhythm. We needn't discuss that now.

FP   No, we've killed that issue, driven a stake through its heart.

MM   But I could quote Chopin and Liszt. You know my favorite quote of Chopin's, *"Suplesse est toute."* Flexibility is everything. Liszt's motto was "Abandon and flexibility." Abandon is spiritual letting go and flexibility is physical letting go. Not surprising that those two should be associated.

FP   This seems to fit with what I recognize as your Zen view, that if you prepare in the right way and are in the right frame of mind, then the doing itself is relatively simple.

MM   That is true. While I found this for myself, I was pleased to find that it was discovered many years earlier.

FP   My number one technical question: As a child, I was instructed to curve my fingers and hit the keys like hammers. What was that all about?

MM   A pedagogic convention that unhappily persists

and has nothing to do with a natural approach to the instrument. It is inhibiting and a great disadvantage. So many of us have been taught that in the beginning. Liszt disliked this approach to the instrument for making the playing dry and mechanical. I think it has to be rejected outright.

FP   Are there other pedagogic conventions popular in the teaching of piano that are ineffective or disruptive?

MM   I'm sure there are many, but a hand in which motion is inhibited or restrained or forced kills musicality. The premise I make is simple. We play the piano by moving, and anything that inhibits, forces, or cramps motion is a tremendous disadvantage. If you allow the freest movement and easiest phrase motion, everything will be fluid, graceful, and relaxed, and won't break the continuity.

FP   That's it then?

MM   Yes, except perhaps we should say a little more about the matter of attitude.

FP   Attitude? Posture?

MM   I mean posture in the broadest sense. I'm concerned with the entire relation one has to the piano and to music, from the physical relation with the instrument to the mental and spiritual relation with the music. The way you sit and move reveals almost everything about your relation to the piano.

We can begin with the physical stance, and that has to do with just sitting correctly. It is as important at the piano as form is in tennis. It may be disadvantageous to stand facing the net in tennis, and at the piano it would be disadvantageous to sit in any way cramped or at the wrong height. Or slumped, with the back broken. One has to sit with the knee an inch or so under the keyboard, and half on the chair, because if the chair is right under one, it pulls one back, and your weight isn't freely available. The forearms should be level, the elbows a little way out from the body, and the hand absolutely unheld, which is not what tradition tells us. We're often told that we should hold the hand in a tight curve, which is a real handicap. Above all, allow the freest uninhibited motion when moving the key and for any lateral motion. Movement should be free, the arm buoyant, the whole body buoyant.

FP   You spoke about anything that inhibits motion. That must include certain mental attitudes.

MM   Yes, I think so. Since you play the piano by moving, and you say that something that is very expressive is very moving, that must include one's mental attitude as much as one's physical attitude. One controls the music by letting go, not by holding on. It is like learning to ride a bicycle. If, for every unintentional tone, we were to fall off the piano bench, we would, in one week have a natural technique. We learn to balance the bicycle easily in about a week, and we discover that holding on is not the key. However pianists are often told to hold the hands or fingers firmly, the beginning of all bad habits.

FP   You use the term "attitude" to describe posture and ability to move. Do you know the popular use of the word "attitude" to mean a "bad attitude" in describing a difficult person?

MM   Of course. Everyone has some sort of attitude. Good or bad. Attitude implies a way of relating to something or someone. Anything forced or predetermined is likely to yield poor results.

FP   What about the notion about a composer's style? Isn't that a predetermined attitude?

MM   It is, and you must be on guard to see that doesn't happen. You should only reflect what is present in the music. To the degree that you are predecided and know how it goes, you have a problem. And, in fact, it does not leave you open to the music, and the odds are that you will have trouble recreating it spontaneously.

FP   I see.

MM   I like Erich Fromm's interpretation of the story of Adam and Eve as an allegory about humankind cut off from nature by knowledge. We long to return to nature and to natural responses to the world or to music. That conflict between the natural and the knowledgeable is inherent in any art. Knowledge is both a help and a hindrance. As an artist you must put knowledge behind you. That's why we value the painting of children. Up to an age of about 13 there may be a wonderful spontaneity, and then there is trouble.

FP   There's a lot of trouble at about the age of 13. That, too, has to do with what happened in the garden of Eden. I do have another question, perhaps about attitude.

MM   You mean one's entire approach to music.

FP   Yes. I wanted to ask about something a bit different — concentration. It seems essential in most activities I know and value.

MM   I couldn't agree more. It's central for anything done at a high level.

FP   Are there students who have trouble concentrating at the piano and then don't do as well?

MM   You could turn it around and get an easier answer. Is there anyone who concentrates absolutely? And the answer would be very few, but the ones who do are great.

FP   And I would imagine that an awareness of an audience could be devastating to concentration.

MM   Exactly. I do believe that one of the merits of the concept of duration is that thinking rhythm so clearly and staying behind the flow is really an exercise in concentration. It tells you where and how to concentrate. I've said to students preparing a recital, if you come to a trepidatious place or you know of a spot that is troubling, try not to think of that, but think of continuity. Think of the rhythm and make that strong. Because the rhythm has everything to do with relationship. And memory relies on association. To try, in an insecure place, to focus on a difficulty is to isolate it, removing it from context and increasing the chance that one will forget.

FP   So concentration is aided by a strong sense of rhythm.

MM   Yes.

FP   Any other techniques for helping concentration?

MM   It is most important to practice conscious awareness. Concentration is also a practice, and nothing is so important as to be thinking of what you do while you are doing it. It is so easy to play automatically, thoughtlessly, and that is a dangerous habit. It is essential to play and practice with intensified consciousness and thoughtfulness. Finally, the focus must be on the music and not on oneself.

FP   Any self-consciousness at all is destructive.

MM   Any great performance has to do with being egoless. There was an interesting review in the *New York Times* about the 98-year-old pianist, Horszowski, who played a wonderful recital, and the reviewer was complimenting him by saying all the things the performance was not. It was not this and not that and so on. He was writing in a backward style. He said that "If technique is power and speed, then the relative quiet of this performance would seem to be a deficiency." Then he went on to say that the performer didn't impose his persona on the music but allowed the music to speak.

FP   That's the goal, isn't it?

MM   That's it.

FP   Are there other questions of technique that we might discuss?

MM   Oh yes. We should say something about finding your way at the keyboard. It really is straightforward. Think about learning to type. The keyboard is complicated, but the students have little trouble learning touch typing with keys that are unlettered. They watch a chart above them and they learn to touch-type. You'd think that pianists who have played for years would do the same. Most pianists believe the visual sense allows them to find the right keys. You can look at a key for a week, and it won't go down. But you can look up at a page and visualize the key and touch. You won't interfere with the sense of the body in space, and that enables you to find and touch and play a key; it is touch that is secure. About 90 percent of the notes you need are already under your hand or are easily within reach of a note you already have in hand. And anyone who glances once at the keyboard, then puts his hands in his lap, looks straight ahead, and lets the hand go to touch the key, will find it. The finger may go glancing off a black key and then find the right one. One should never sound a tone without first being in touch and taking time to touch. Touch cues are learned very quickly. You can find your way by touch. You must

test this with utter consistency. Think to touch and touch
to think. Learn to rely on the sense of touch and visualize
the key. To start, take a new piece, somewhat simple, and
go slowly. Tell yourself you will not look, no matter how
long you take to find the keys, but do it entirely by touch.
Then you will be surprised how quickly you learn and
how secure it will be.

FP   Mort, what should I do with wrong notes? It
seems that I have at least two possibilities. One is to
replay the measure or the phrase or the wrong note.
Sometimes it seems necessary. And yet, to maintain the
sense of flow, maybe I just ought go on.

MM   There is a wonderful passage in the book of conversations with Claudio Arrau. The questioner asked
about people minding wrong notes. And Arrau answered
that it was their privilege, the privilege of genius, to have
wrong notes. He went on to say that Edwin Fischer was a
very great pianist but couldn't possibly record today
because they would ask him to record over and over to
take out the wrong notes, and he couldn't possibly do it.
And then he went on to describe Ansorge, a fine pianist
who played *nothing* but wrong notes.

   But I think it has to do with your aim in practicing.
If you are trying to get a sense of the whole thing and of
the continuity overall, you have to go on, not stopping to
repair. But there surely is a time in practicing when you
have to allow no wrong notes at all. Think it correctly, go
slowly enough and carefully to right a passage that may
be going off. Otherwise, correctness should not be the
determining thing. It was Richter who said that American

pianists are much too concerned with mechanical accuracy. I think that is true. Everyone knows that mass-produced regularity is not preferable to hand-crafted pottery, but in the recording industry that influence is pernicious; the aesthetic of the technician has taken over, and people are quite convinced that mechanical accuracy comes before all else.

FP   In Mexico, hand-crafted pottery with flaws is pointed out with pride as *hecho a mano*. So wrong notes are not reasons for suicide or chopping up the piano or taking up another hobby?

MM   No. You have to think of what is most important. Having every last syllable in place and enunciation with perfection will rob a statement of meaning.

You know, we've talked about the relaxed hand, but we should also consider the relaxed wrist. We're all told that it is advisable that the wrist be relaxed. And of course, it is true for wrist, elbows, fingers. But how to know how relaxed to be? You can take your other hand to gently lift your wrist perhaps half an inch, just to see if you can catch a bit of unsuspected tension. Such checking will help you step outside of habit and play with increasing suppleness and freedom.

FP   I don't know what to do with that. Partly I don't believe it.

MM   Why not?

FP   After all, there must be a degree of tautness in every part of your arm and hand.

MM   Of course, but if you perform any action and are as relaxed as possible, you accomplish it most efficiently. You can discover that your fingers can be playing even though the wrist is loose.

FP   Maybe so, because the finger flexors do start at the elbow, but they go through a sort of pulley system at the wrist. I suppose you could ask the finger flexor to compensate for any wrist motion. But a bit of control of the wrist seems to make it easier.

MM   All right. But if you practice, perhaps some Hanon, you could test the idea about wrist flexibility and relaxedness and see that it helps attain the utmost relaxedness.

FP   I think that I threw all my Hanon out. Some-where in the past I decided that I could live the rest of my life quite satisfactorily without ever trying to do Hanon again.

MM   I can sympathize with that. But if you use it cor-rectly, you can learn a tremendous amount with Hanon, but not the way we ordinarily play him, which is as a mechanical exercise. It is a convenient set with which to examine your approach and to make even the simplest patterns musical.

FP   Is Hanon music?

MM   You should play Hanon or any technique so that it is in no way unmusical. One should have a fine tone, a line, and above all, continuity. If there is an honest tone as well, it will be musical. And if the tone is exactly what you intend, it will sound beautiful.

FP   I have a few other "How do you" questions. For example, how does one approach the problem of different rhythms in the bass and treble? For example four notes in the treble matching up with a triplet in the bass?

MM   The best way of working out that problem is to play, alternately, the shortest segment between two points that match in the two rhythms. If you have to match five to seven, you play the five-note passage and then the seven-note passage, several times separately, and then put them together. Curiously, five and six will match up more easily than three and four. That works better than finding the lowest common multiple. You must hold the starting points and ending points and the common duration. If you have three and four, you try that at first, and then try with two groups, six and eight. That will work for you.

FP   Are there other common questions that you are asked of a "How do I do this" sort?

MM   Yes. One common puzzle is how to play one hand softer than the other. I suggest doing the two hands separately. First the melody, with exactly the color you wish. Then the other hand, softly, but with the same intensity. Then go back and forth a bit, and when you put them together, you will be playing with equal intensity but a difference in volume.

FP   I see. I have been playing the second impromptu in Schubert's second set. The melody is the top note of the chords played in the right hand. It doesn't help to practice one hand alone.

MM   Well, it helps to divide the right hand part between the two hands. Play the melody with the right hand and the balance of the chord with the left. When playing it all together, as written, think the melody very strongly because intention is so very important. You would have to have heard Myra Hess, the British pianist, who would play such works as encores, to imagine how warm and singing a tone can be. Only a creative imagination, total relaxation and tremendous energy can achieve an approximate copy of her unique tone. Her playing of similar works, for example the Brahms A flat Waltz, put much more famous artists in the shade.

FP   And yet there are pieces where I can't find the melody and still enjoy them. The third movement of the seventh Prokofiev sonata seems like that.

MM   No, the line is there: bright, taut, incisive, using a deep touch. Not too broad a line. He is always singing.

FP   Given all that, I still have trouble finding the line. I guess that if I ever find it, it will have those characteristics.

MM   At the beginning, it is in the top. The tune is very marked, sometimes very prominent. Athletic.

FP   How do you memorize?

MM   I suggest that you take about three steps. Look at
a measure or two. Think the sound. Fold your hands,
look at the page, and think the sound very clearly. The
keyboard and the sound are all in your mind. Do that a
couple of times, maybe play a note you can't image clearly. Then, close your eyes or look away, and see if you can
repeat the process without the page. If you have to, go
back and see where you are stuck. Do that over and over
until you can think the sound and the keyboard. Then
play by memory. It is very conscious. Just the opposite of
that unconscious memorization that the very young and
the very gifted can rely upon. The ability to think tone
clearly is the basis for a secure memory, and you
strengthen the conscious association with the keyboard.
The easy memorizers are those with the best inner ear.

FP   A related question, can one teach to play by ear?

MM   I think it is an ability that can be cultivated. It is
often a gift. But you can cultivate it, too. Nothing will
help build a musical technique so much as learning to listen and learning to think tone.

/ /

Balances: An Aesthetic for the Pianist

Creation means the bringing form out of the void.
~ Ferruccio Busoni

MM   What we need is a unifying aesthetic for the pianist. You probably realize that if you do not have a conscious aesthetic you must have an unconscious one, but it won't be better for that and possibly worse.

FP   OK. What do you have in mind?

MM   I was thinking that a useful aesthetic will allow you to achieve more yet do less. Busoni said, "Know nothing but rather think and feel." However, achieving more will involve some thinking. Look at the following scheme, which attempts to put all we have talked about in a clear relation.

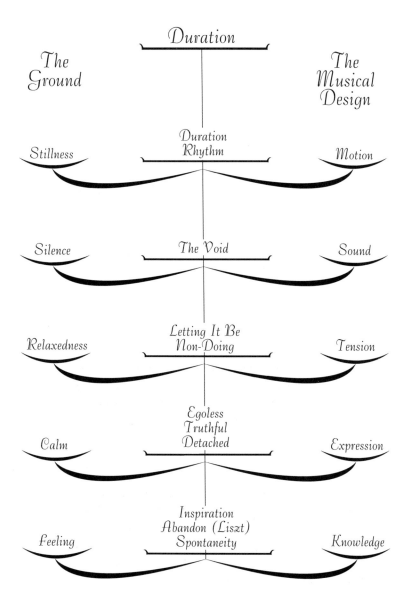

Fig. 1
Balances

FP   It seems to have all your favorite terms!

MM   Right! Notice the central points. If you understand that these result when resolving conflicting elements, you will be able to simplify and focus energy. The
essentials to keep in mind are:

Duration

The Void

Non-doing or Letting be

Honest expression

Spontaneity

          These arise when combining conflicting elements.
Motion, tone, and expression are the positive elements.
What is, is defined by what is not. I am not the first to
find this out, as you know. You would not understand
motion if you could not be still, nor could you perceive
tone but for silence, perform any action effectively without relaxing the inactive muscles, nor use knowledge
wisely unless guided by musical instinct.

FP   So the midpoints are not a balance as much as a
combining of disparate elements. I think that your diagram is a little bit confusing because you mean it to serve
two purposes, to show balances of opposites and to
show a way of combining opposites.

MM   Yes. We probably need two diagrams. However, when you combine these opposites you arrive at a synthesis that contains both. This is not an intellectual exercise but an experience best understood while recreating a musical work. Our concern is usually with the active side of the equation, with tone, movement, and expression. You can reach a higher level if you are equally attentive to the quite still side, that is the negative or the ground. Expression is stronger against absolute calm. Tone is more defined against a silence. Motion perceived in a still space will create suspense or duration.

FP   Mmm. So you think that combining the ideas of stillness and motion lets one come up with the feeling of duration?

MM   Yes, that is what I think, in brief.

FP   How about not so brief?

MM   Well, the pianist Edward Steurmann described the composer Arnold Schoenberg as a wonderful conductor because he could make music seem to move and stand still at the same time. This is the sense of duration, and it is the basis for every beautiful performance. Sviatoslov Richter's teacher, Neuhaus, said that he had heard all the "great ones," but that he thought Richter was unique for his sense of what he termed "Time-Rhythm." I think he is describing an awareness of duration. Pablo Casals, in his book *Conversations*, says that without this sense of "time in space" no artist will reach the highest level. All this seems to say that duration is fundamental. Of course, there is no accepted term or easy explanation of just what duration is.

FP   I need to go back. Looking at this figure that shows a series of scales hanging from duration, I find the first focal point suspended below is also labeled duration. So duration is both the overall single principle upon which everything hangs and also ...

MM   I mean to say that without rhythm, the rest will fall.

FP   All hangs on rhythm. But when you look at rhythm itself, you say that it is a combination of motion and stillness. A balance. The sum of these two elements?

MM   Do you regard the resolution of opposites as a sum? If so, the result would be nothing.

FP   I don't know. Maybe there is another way of combining two elements than addition. Multiplication? The combination you describe then, a "resolution of opposites," implies that it still contains both opposites.

MM   Absolutely.

FP   And when you contain both original elements, do you go to a new place? Are you at something different?

MM   Yes. The mid-point represents a new and different place.

FP Well, let's move on to the next balance, that between the tone and silence.

MM It should be evident that listening to the silence will make the sound more telling. The silence needs to be as solid as the sound; the result then is a seamless shape. I like Busoni's statement that creativity comes out of the void. You have to be willing to deal with nothing. A proper silence will be as expressive as the adjoining sounds.

FP I'm uncomfortable with the term you use for the resolution of tone and silence. You call it "the void?"

MM Yes. An alternative term would be "a musical form," created out of the void.

FP OK. How about the next balance?

MM That is tension and activity with relaxedness and passivity. Performing any action involves tension: you must relax other muscles in order to move easily. If you want to play with all possible energy you will find that you must relax yet more, an obvious contradiction. Finally, you will be able to play with great energy yet easily, apparently relaxed, literally embodying these opposites.

FP Which is harder? The activity? Or the passive letting go?

MM I think the latter. Especially in our culture.

FP   So one has to work harder at the passive element?

MM   No, you must play more easily! But with all your might.

FP   And expression-calm?

MM   Opposed to expression or emotion are calm or non-emotion. Their resolution is in being detached, egoless, and truthful. That attitude is expressed by the German *verfremdung* (estrangement), used by Bertolt Brecht, or my term, bemused. If expression is not forced and comes out of a serene setting, it will be an honest statement. Nor will you place yourself between the music and the listener. Rather you will be a direct channel for the music conveyed without interference to the listener.

FP   Are there professional pianists who are the opposite?

MM   There are pianists who believe that what *they* are expressing is more important than what the music says, but they are not the great ones.

FP   What about the last of the opposites?

MM   That is the balance between thinking and feeling, and between knowledge and instinct. You cannot play out of your head only, nor can it be an outpouring of feeling alone. You must reconcile both sides of this equation. The resolution is expressed in my motto, Let It Be. Curiously it was some time before I realized that Liszt meant almost the same thing with his motto, *Abandon*. Let the music and let yourself be; the music should be neither restrained nor forced.

FP   Letting things happen. Being ready for anything and letting it happen. Sometimes it feels as if something magic happened. Being ready is one thing, but when it happens, it feels magical.

MM   That's right. It is magic because you create an illusion that the piano can speak or sing and that it can express joy, sorrow, or any emotion.

FP   Do you think that feeling is in the doing or in the experiencing?

MM   I believe it is both. It has to be. If you mean whether it is in performer or listener, the answer is the same. It is in both.

FP   For me, most of the time both are the same person. Most of the time I am my only listener. Sometimes I play a piece well and then look around to see if anyone else heard it and there is no one. Just me.

MM   Yes, we are really drawing in thin air, and it vanishes immediately.

FP   So, in summary, this diagram of the active and passive elements ...

MM   Points to the contradictions, to be resolved on

another level. That resolution will elevate all your playing.

FP   And what is the reason to keep these contradictions clear in your mind?

MM   It allows you to get into that still place where you can be the person doing it yet be the person watching. And it allows you to balance all the elements. It prevents overstatement. It keeps you from going off on a tangent. As students and later as pianists, we are prey to the last idea, the last perception that has become clear. In resolving these contradictory elements, we are able to keep a right balance and reach a higher level. First and last, it accords rhythm, rightly understood, its proper place as the all-inclusive element affecting the whole design.

12

Teaching Piano

What I have learned from Leschetitsky I am unable to say, to estimate, to appreciate. He succeeded in releasing all the vitality and elan and sense of beauty a student had in his nature; and would not tolerate any deviation or violation of what he felt to be truthfulness of expression.

~ Artur Schnabel

FP   Mort, how did you become a teacher of piano?

MM   I think I learned by doing it. I started when still in my teens as an assistant to the music teacher at the Ojai Valley School. Later on, when studying with Mildred Couper in Santa Barbara, I taught some of her students, when she was composer-in-residence at the McDowell Colony.

FP   What did you do?

MM   Well, it was helping them practice, going over the music they were preparing. I can't remember how well it worked, just that I did it. I didn't realize that it would be a life's work, nor that I would develop any special gift as a teacher.

FP   When did you think that?

MM   When I had moved to Palo Alto in the '40s and had begun to teach professionally and was performing, I saw that concepts that helped the playing applied in the teaching. And in those days, just as I played, I taught. I played out of instinct and inspiration which was what I thought was important and was how I taught. Even then, and before, I had already begun keeping notebooks where I wrote down any insight or concept that could explain what was happening when playing was at its best. Teaching spontaneity or inspiration seems improbable; nevertheless I got people to go beyond themselves at any level, and I could see that it was possible. Do you know what I mean by "going beyond themselves?"

FP   Improving?

MM   More than improving. I would expect them to make a leap to another level. They could do that, those who were musical. And that was what I expected of myself. I don't teach quite like that now, perhaps a pity, but more sensibly.

FP   Not to expect quantum leaps?

MM   I still expect that, but it is more solidly grounded now. It does come out of knowledge as well as instinct, and I make it clear that the key is rhythm. But in those days it was very instinctive. And it would happen. Almost everyone would do quite marvelous playing, and I expected that.

FP   What about those other few? I always feel myself to be an untalented pianist. I'm in that other group.

MM   That is not true. I believe that it is human to be musical and musical to be human. Everyone is musical to some degree. Dancing and singing, or rather, moving and speaking, are basic to our existence. If that musical nature is expressed, you can learn to play beautifully. You may not be able to play big works or an entire program for hundreds, but you will be able to choose a composition from the huge literature for the piano and play that beautifully. Inspired playing is not only the special province of famous artists. The amateur can bring enthusiasm and spontaneity that may be lacking for the professional because of the pressure and routine of the concert business. Commercialization puts an unhealthy premium on tidy packaging and mechanical perfection, and that is an added burden for the professional concert pianist.

FP   So I shouldn't think that I was one of those few who couldn't make great strides forward?

MM   Not at all. I know that you can. No rationalization will allow you to make a simple line into a musical statement. It always has to be a creation and then a re-creation. The student comes to understand that everyone has the capacity to play creatively.

FP   I would like to go back to something you said.

Initially you didn't think of teaching as an art and a talent.
Do you now?

MM   I do. I was fortunate to have studied with exceptional teachers. Richard Buhlig in Los Angeles, Mildred
Couper in Santa Barbara, Alexander Raab and Bernhard
Abramowitsch in Berkeley were outstanding pianists and
musicians. Both Raab and Buhlig were Leschetitsky
pupils. Couper had studied with Alfred Cortot.
Abramowitsch was a fine artist himself and my most
important teacher with whom I studied last and longest.
However my ability to conceptualize and to set goals that
are somewhat visionary enables students to change dramatically and to make those leaps I described earlier.

FP   What is your idea of good teaching?

MM   It is the opposite of the classic Svengali syndrome
which is to make the teacher indispensable. My goal is to
make the teacher dispensable. You learn what the musical goals are, to trust your own judgement and ability,
and finally to recognize that there is no outer authority,
only inner resources and musical integrity. My goal as
teacher is the same as pianist, to do the least possible to
achieve the best results. A good teacher is a good shep-
herd. To the degree I am successful, it is in releasing the
student's inherent musical nature. I don't say "faster
here, louder there, slower here." Students come to the
realization that they can decide what feels right. An honest and convincing statement grows from their interaction with the work they are studying. In that sense I don't
teach at all. I just point the way. And the ideal would be

to do that, saying and doing the least possible, just as in playing that should be one's goal.

FP   I see. Do the least possible, but just at the right place. I recently spent a week learning about how to coach doctors to better talk with patients. Thinking about coaches I've worked with and of you as a coach, I realized that you made the musical goal clear. That is, you talked more about the music and what we desired to produce and less about the mechanics of playing the piano. I wonder if that is a requirement of successful coaching, to clearly define the goal?

MM   Yes, if it's the right goal. I like to teach last things first, in effect making distant goals very immediate. The problem for the teacher is that one discovers the last things at the last. But I always have found that things you might think only an advanced artist would be concerned with may be explained at any level. And I have had great results with that. Nothing should be held back. The ability to play an express silence is a good example. The concept of playing a silence seems quite abstract at first. If rightly understood it becomes very concrete for even the less advanced.

FP   What seemed the most important to you in your teaching?

MM   Inspiration! An out-of-fashion term, I know. Literally to breathe life into something or someone, so it is a proper expression. I saw that students at every level could capture the spirit in the music, and they and the music would be transformed. It seemed magical. While it was important for the student, my estimate of the place for inspiration changed. I realized at a later time the merit of Busoni's rule for practice, "Never be carried away by inspiration." Nonetheless, inspiration gave both students and myself confidence in playing and in one's own musicality, and I was able to release this gift in others.

FP   And was that sense of inspiration enough?

MM   Well, at first, I thought so. I believed everything was accomplished, and only at a later time I realized that was the place to start practicing, that insight would be transitory unless it was more solidly grounded. Once I had learned the notes, studied the piece and practiced it, I had a tendency to think everything else came through inspiration. Later I concluded that you should not practice for inspiration but rather be inspired to practice.

FP   I wonder if "inspiration" really describes the end result. Sort of like "being happy." An admirable goal but not the route to it.

MM   I think so! Now I say, "Don't copy the result but try to see how you got there." Was it paying attention to time, to line, what? Then you know what to attend to the next time."

FP   Suppose I tell you how I saw you as a teacher and see if it sounds at all like the person you thought you were.

MM   All right.

FP   I found you to be a different sort of teacher from any I had experienced before.

MM   I hope so.

FP   I thought of you as kind, supportive, and caring. You taught more about the music than the piano. At times it seemed very confusing. Sometimes I would go home and tell my wife that I had no idea what I had just been told, but I thought that I had enjoyed it.

MM   So you want to know if that is how I see myself? Well, one who illumines music, gives direction, and indicates to the students that they can tell what is right. I would like you to feel that you can trust your own judgement, that there is no outer authority and that you trust your musical nature. And to discriminate between what is a truthful expression and what is false.

FP   That is the result you would like.

MM   Yes.

FP   And the teacher's characteristics that lead to that are ...

MM   I see myself as an open person, one who loves discussion, who is honest, and who is supportive. Patience; that's my stock in trade. Someone who is kind and who can transmit love of music. I set almost impossible standards, yet am very relaxed about their realization. I never set myself above the least talented, and I am never threatened by the most gifted. And I love humor; I even have a bit of it.

FP   I have been thinking about the abuse that teachers often heap upon their students. Even in medical school, even now. I remember it well from thirty years ago. It was the norm to humiliate and punish the student. Part of it was a sort of hazing and part a theory of pedagogy.

MM   All too often true, and what an abysmal theory it is.

FP   Yes, and I believe a model that can be found in music. Great conductors are often noted for their harshness, I think.

MM   Not so much nowadays. Perhaps Reiner, Toscanini, and Szell in the past.

FP   That never seemed to be your style though.

MM   No, of course. The teacher should teach at the student's level. An insecure teacher tends to be or feel superior and to trust in method, or rule, or structure. Rather, trust the student. How else will students learn to trust in themselves?

FP   So it is a mistake to focus too much on the way the material should be played at the expense of the student.

MM   Surely. For the student is also the material. I teach human beings, not only music. Imagine that you are forming your vision of a beautiful bowl on a potter's wheel. The clay is too soft and, because you do not take that into account, it crumbles. Recognize and accept your material. The result may be even better than expected.

FP   I wonder how you came to that teaching approach.

MM   Probably by temperament and experience and possibly the influence of the Ojai Valley School. At that time it was a progressive school, in the best sense, that cultivated the best in the student. There were remarkable teachers for whom I remain grateful.

FP   You know, I was tempted to ask you if you thought of music and teaching music as a sort of therapy.

MM   If you mean do I alter the student's musical life? The answer would be yes. While I am very attuned to the student's feelings, I certainly don't consider myself a musical therapist. I know the student will be forever changed; perception, technique, and musicality will never be the same. They will be confident of their own musical nature and see and hear the big picture. That is what makes piano playing musical and music meaningful.

FP   Has teaching been fulfilling for you?

MM   There have been great rewards in teaching. One of the happiest rewards is that many students have remained lifelong friends. And that is something you couldn't have bargained for.

FP   Can you sum up your approach to teaching the piano?

MM   I think it best to go from the general to the particular. First the main idea and then the detail, never losing sight of the whole. The deepest understanding comes from seeing the whole design. Students develop best if you *Let Them Be*. Trust in their capacity and musicality. Just as they will do best moving freely physically, so will they if they are free intellectually and spiritually. Young pianists will be free to develop and grow and express what they genuinely feel in the music they play.

FP   Mort, what is the meaning of life?

MM   I like best the answer that Vikor Frankl, the existentialist psychiatrist gave. He said that we shouldn't ask the question. Life asks us the question and that our life is the answer. That answer has always comforted me.

About the Authors

Mortimer Markoff

Mortimer Markoff is a native Californian, born in Los Angeles and raised in Southern California. His Russian-born parents established dairy farms, first in Arcadia and then in the Ojai Valley where they moved so that Mort could attend the Ojai Valley School. Mort began studying the piano at age eight and then continued in his early teens, studying first with Elizabeth Price Coffey, then with Richard Buhlig in Los Angeles, and later with Mildred Couper in Santa Barbara. His first recitals were during his study with Mildred Couper.

Mort first taught piano as an assistant coach for the instructor in music at the Ojai Valley School. He then moved on to the University of California as a music student. While in Berkeley, he studied piano with Alexander

Raab and then with Bernhard Abramowitsch.

The second World War interrupted his university study, and for several years Mort did marine construction work. As a member of S.F. Local 34, the Pile Drivers' Union, he worked for Henry Kaiser, and later he worked as a shipwright outfitting Liberty ships at Kaiser's Richmond shipbuilding yards. Throughout this period he continued private study with Abramowitsch, working days and practicing the piano evenings.

Mort married in 1942 and settled in Palo Alto where he established himself as a pianist and teacher with successful professional debuts in Palo Alto and San Francisco. He has one son and two daughters and has lived in Palo Alto for the last fifty years.

In the '70s, he completed his academic work at the College of Notre Dame and San Francisco State University, earning a Masters' Degree in composition, having studied with Roger Nixon and Andrew Imbrie.

He has taught on the faculties of the College of Notre Dame and Foothill College, presented workshops, and lectured for the California Music Teachers' Association. He has taught classes, groups, and individuals from beginner to master level. Much of his teaching has been devoted to teachers of piano, thus earning him a reputation as a master teacher.

Fred Platt

Growing up in Chicago, Fred Platt studied piano with Ottolie Bauer from age eight to thirteen. He attended public shcools in Chicago, then Northwestern

University, graduating with a BA and MA in mathematics. He married Connie McCormick, and the two moved to California where he was a medical student at Stanford. Graduating in 1964, he conducted postgraduate work in internal medicine at the University of Chicago and Presbyterian Medical Center in Denver. From 1966 to 1968, he served in the infantry as an army doctor.

Fred worked in the Denver General Hospital emergency department from 1970 to 1973, and wrote the textbook *Case Studies in Emergency Medicine*. He then directed the medical residency at Presbyterian Medical Center from 1973 to 1981 and since has practiced general internal medicine in Denver. He is known as an expert on the problems in communication that doctors and patients experience together and is the author of a text on communication, *Conversation Failure*, published by Life Sciences Press.

In 1960, he met Mortimer Markoff, with whom he studied for two years. They have been good friends ever since.

ORDER FORM

YES, PLEASE SEND ME _____
COPIES OF 'THE ART OF
PLAYING THE PIANO.'

❑ SINGLE COPY @ $14.95
  add $2.00 shipping/handling per book.

❑ 5 - 9 COPIES @ $12.95
  add $1.00 shipping/handling per book.

❑ 10+ COPIES @ $10.95
  add $1.00 shipping/handling per book.

Colorado residents should add sales tax.

❑ CHECK ENCLOSED
❑ MONEY ORDER ENCLOSED

$_____AMOUNT TOTAL

PLEASE SEND MY BOOK(S) TO:

_____
NAME

_____
ADDRESS

_____

_____
TELEPHONE

PLEASE PHOTOCOPY AND FILL OUT THIS FORM,
ENCLOSE YOUR PAYMENT AND SEND TO:

PIANO DIALOGUES
396 STEELE STREET,
DENVER, CO 80206